FISH TALES
(From the Belly of the Whale)

For comments or questions about this book,
visit our website: *The Lost Stories Channel*,
at loststorieschannel.com

© 2017 by W. Kent Smith – All Rights Reserved
Published in the United States
by Lodestar Cinema Creations
West Covina, California
Smith, W. Kent (1959-)

It should be noted that this book contains
exactly the same material from a larger work of
the same title, and as such differs only in that
this version presents Reel One of Three.

Front Cover and Title Page Painting:
Jonah and the Whale, Pieter Lastman, 1621

Book Exterior and Interior
Designed and Executed
by W. Kent Smith

All the artwork for this book is in the public
domain and is therefore not subject to
copyright infringement.

No part of this book may be reproduced in any
form without the prior written consent of the
publisher, except in brief quotations embodied
in critical articles and reviews.

ISBN: 978-0-9675869-7-7

Manufactured in the U.S.A.
April 2017

Fish Tales
(From the Belly of the Whale)

Fifty of the Greatest Misconceptions
Ever Blamed on The Bible

REEL ONE
The Hook
#50-34

by

W. Kent Smith

Books by W. Kent Smith

Lies My Professor Told Me About American Politics: Questions Concerning the Original Vision of the Founding Fathers

Conquering Cynicism in a Modern Age: How The Bible in Nature Provides an Antidote to Doubt and Despair

On Earth as It is On Heaven: The Promise of America, Technology, and the New Earth, Book One, The Promise of America

The Book of Days: In Search of the 5,500-year Prophecy Given to Adam About the Coming of Christ

The Book of Tales: Stories That Confirm the 5,500-year Prophecy Given to Adam About the Coming of Christ

Fish Tales (From the Belly of the Whale): Fifty of the Greatest Misconceptions Ever Blamed on The Bible, Reel One, The Hook #50-34

Fish Tales (From the Belly of the Whale): Fifty of the Greatest Misconceptions Ever Blamed on The Bible, Reel Two, The Line #33-18

Fish Tales (From the Belly of the Whale): Fifty of the Greatest Misconceptions Ever Blamed on The Bible, Reel Three, The Sinker #17-1

Fish Tales (From the Belly of the Whale): Fifty of the Greatest Misconceptions Ever Blamed on The Bible, The Complete Edition, Hook, Line, and Sinker #50-1

Tales of Forever: The Unfolding Drama of God's Hidden Hand in History, Book One: The Analyses – Part One

Tales of Forever: The Unfolding Drama of God's Hidden Hand in History, Book Two: The Tales – Part One

Tales of Forever: The Unfolding Drama of God's Hidden Hand in History, Book Three: The Tales – Part Two

Tales of Forever: The Unfolding Drama of God's Hidden Hand in History, Book Four: The Analyses – Part Two

Tales of Forever: The Unfolding Drama of God's Hidden Hand in History, The Complete Edition

For my Kids,

Ever loving, ever faithful

Contents

An Unrelenting Search 1

The Mirror of Truth 3

Turning Light into Darkness 5

Concepts in Misconceptions 8

From the Least to the Greatest 13

REEL ONE
The Hook #50-34

Misconception #50
*Before the Tower of Babel,
Everyone Spoke Just One Language* 17

Misconception #49
All the Curses Inflicted by God are Perpetual in Nature 22

Misconception #48
*When the Disciples Asked Jesus
When He'd Establish His Kingdom,
He Said They'd Have to Wait Till the End of the Age* 27

Misconception #47
*The Israelites were Always Slaves
in Egypt Until Moses Led Them Out of Bondage* 34

Misconception #46
*God Sent Serpents After the Children of Israel
as They Wandered Through the Wilderness* 41

Misconception #45
*When Abraham Sought to Sacrifice Him, Isaac was
Still a Child With No Idea What His Father was Planning* 47

Misconception #44
Moses Spent Forty Years as a Lonely Shepherd Before He Led Israel in the Exodus 53

Misconception #43
Only Humans Get into Heaven; Sorry, No Pets Allowed 59

Misconception #42
All Students of The Zodiac are Fools or Heretics 66

Misconception #41
Jesus was Just a Poor Carpenter's Son Before His Real Ministry Began 74

Misconception #40
Mary the Mother of Jesus was Born Via a Virgin Birth Just Like Her Son 79

Misconception #39
When Jesus Commended a Person for Offering Water to the Least of His Brothers, He Meant It to Anyone in Need 86

Misconception #38
When Jesus' Listeners Demanded a Sign, He Told Them No More Signs from God Would be Given 90

Misconception #37
Jesus was Born on December 25th 95

Misconception #36
Jesus Never Answered Pilate's Question: "What is Truth?" 103

Misconception #35
The Call of Christ Comes Unexpectedly and Unannounced 108

Misconception #34
Not Even God Can Find the Lost Tribes of Israel 114

Coming Attractions
Reel Two: The Line #33-18 123

About the Author
.... 124

FISH TALE:
An improbable story that alludes to the tendency of fishermen to exaggerate the size of their catch; figuratively, a great big lie.

An Unrelenting Search

YOU BELIEVE *The Bible* is the inspired word of God, but can you always tell the difference between a genuine message from it and a counterfeit version? Take, for example, the following truths that are said to come straight from Holy Writ. Which of them would you say are genuine and which would you say are counterfeit?

Jesus was just a poor carpenter's son before His real ministry began.

Only humans get into Heaven; sorry, no pets allowed.

Jesus was born on December 25th.

Theology and science are natural enemies because of their inherent incompatibility.

Hell, like Heaven, is a place of perpetual existence.

Nobody knows the day or the hour of the Second Coming of Christ, not even Jesus.

The verse: "Wives submit to your husbands" is a one-way street.

"An eye for an eye and a tooth for a tooth" tells us God demands punishment in every case without exception.

"Slaves obey your masters" proves that slavery is biblically sanctioned and therefore God-ordained.

If you're like most people, you'd probably say they're all genuine, right? But actually, they're some of the greatest misconceptions ever blamed on *The Bible*, because as it turns out, all of these so-called "truths" are false. That is to say, they are if you look to the Scriptures to verify such things.

To that end, *Fish Tales (From the Belly of the Whale)* plunges you headlong into an unrelenting search for biblical truth that will forever change how you think about the word of God. Along the way, you'll discover that *Fish Tales* not only exposes the origins of such misconceptions, but it also restores *The Bible*'s original message of hope and inspiration, which once made it humanity's brightest light in a darkened world.

The Mirror of Truth

IT'S BEEN SAID that confession is good for the soul. If that's true, then I'd like to make my confession, here and now. When I look in the mirror, I'm never quite sure about what I see. Is it the face of a fearless seeker of truth, or of one afraid of embracing the truth? I can't help wondering: What is it about a person that causes them to eagerly run toward the light one day and then eagerly flee from it the next? Why do I find myself abandoning the truth that so often rescues me just when I need it most?

But wait. Could there be another reason why I'm so divided? Is it because *The Bible* often creates as much confusion as it does clarity? After all, it's not only the source of the very best that humanity can offer the world, but it can also be the source of the very worst. And how is that even possible, anyway? Does that mean there's a better way to interpret its message? And if so, am I alone in the search for this better way or actually one among many? Certainly I'm not the first person to ask the question: What is truth? And I'm certainly not the last to wonder why no one bothered to offer an answer.

Then it dawns on me: Maybe we *were* told the answer, but we didn't like the answer we were given. So, when we ask how *The Bible* can inspire both the best and worst in humanity, maybe the problem doesn't lie so much with the book itself but with something altogether different. But what?

Or should I say ... who?

Of course, the Scriptures describe the role that many have played in this great whodunit of the ages. Naturally, there's God. There is—if you believe *The Bible*—the devil. There are the myriad ones who've made their way across the stage of biblical history: Adam and Eve; and Cain and Abel; there's Noah and his family, and Abraham and his descendants; Moses, the prophets; Jesus and the apostles. And just like every great story, each of these timeless tales has a hero and a villain. More often than not, though, while it's easy to blame all our problems on the devil for his role in humanity's downfall, or God for letting it happen, it turns out that the real villain is us.

When we look in the mirror of truth, in those moments when we're being perfectly honest with ourselves, what do we see but two faces staring back at us? No doubt this is the source of many a cartoon where we see an angel sitting on someone's shoulder and a demon sitting on the other while the torn soul in the middle wrestles with the irrefutable logic of what's being whispered into either ear.

The idea is as old as the story of the Garden of Eden. Eve gazed thoughtfully at the Forbidden Fruit in her hand, knowing full well she shouldn't eat it. But right there in her ear was the voice of reason, whispering innocently: "Did God *really* mean what He said?"

Of course, we insist that, given the same opportunity, we'd have done things differently. We'd never make the same mistake she and Adam made—if given the chance, that is.

So what did God do? He figured out how to call our bluff, so that every day and every hour, we *are* faced with the same dilemma. We're faced with having to make a choice between the advice that we're hearing in one ear or the other. "This is the right path." "No, this is it." "Are you *sure* God said to go this way?"

And sadly, because we're all made of the same stuff as our first parents, we, who insist we'd do things differently, end up betraying our own cause, just as they did. The Apostle Paul described our dilemma quite eloquently:

> I've discovered this principle in life—that although I want to do what's right, I inevitably do what's wrong. I love God's Law with all my heart, but there's another power within me that's at war with my mind.[1]

Yes, Satan, as the voice in one ear, does all he can to shipwreck our lives; and yes, God, as the voice in the other ear, does all He can to steer us clear. But guess what, folks? We're still the only ones to blame for repeating the same mistakes that were made so long ago.

But all is not lost. Because in looking at this age-old drama, this inevitable chain of events doesn't spell the end of us. In the hands of the eternal God of redemption, we find ourselves on a new path that teaches us something we could never have learned had we not failed so miserably to begin with. Thus, the end of ourselves, which seemed like such a tragedy at first, actually winds up acting as the prelude for a transformation of biblical proportions.

It's to just such a journey of discovery, then, that I invite all those who've ever asked the same questions that I have: What makes *The Bible* so easy to misinterpret? What forces conspire against us to complicate matters? And what can we do to counteract those forces in order to lay hold of the truth that's literally staring us in the face?

---

[1] *Romans* 7:21-23

Turning Light into Darkness

ONE OF THE MOST famous pictures in Scripture is that of Jesus calling His disciples to follow Him and become "fishers of men."[2] But as marvelous as this scene is—one that speaks of a God Who is ever seeking to save the lost—there's also an ominous flipside; another fisherman is just as determined to fill his boat with fish. That fisherman is Satan; and he has his own crew of fishermen, the children of disobedience in every age, who love darkness more than light.

Whereas Jesus and His crew fish for men with words of truth, Satan and his bunch snag their prey with words of deceit—a succulent bait which disguises the hook that spells the end of any and all unsuspecting fish.

It's this competition, then, between truth and lies, between God and Satan, between two factions of fishermen, that lies at the heart of this story. A whopper of a fish tale, it is, however, not a fish tale in the usual sense, though it does contain certain elements of the tall tale. But in this case, these elements are not interjected to brag but to supply an antidote to the devil's hook of lies. Any exaggeration or distortion of truth in this tale will be engaged strictly to demonstrate the difference between the original form of truth and its refashioned counterpart.

What we're talking about is none other than the truth that the Lord of the Sea Himself has given to His fishermen: *The Bible*.

In the hands of Jesus' fishermen, God's word is a hearty tool that elicits the most cherished commodity in creation—*trust*, or, as it's expressed in biblical terms, *faith*. "Without faith," the Scriptures tell us, "it's impossible to please God."[3] By faith, the ancients parted the waters, raised the dead, and opened the gates of Heaven. Naturally, something this precious to God is the greatest threat to the prince of this world, Satan, who never stops trying to thwart this truth-affirming, faith-creating word of God.

Yet ironically, the one thing the devil has going for him in his quest—the only thing, really—is that contained within the very nature of God's word is a peculiar conundrum. The word is presented to

---

[2] *Matthew* 4:19; *Mark* 1:17

[3] *Hebrews* 11:6

humanity in the form of a paradox, designed not only to reveal the ways of God but also to conceal them. This is done, according to the edict of Heaven, to allow access to the things of God to the faithful while at the same time to bar access to thieves and robbers. Unfortunately, though, that means the very tool that God uses to spark His rescue effort of humanity also contains the slimmest of potentials with which the enemies of God can nullify that divine effort.

It's this double-edged nature of *The Bible*, then, that lies at the heart our dilemma, and why we're so often faced with two apparently opposing realities inspired by a single source. That's why it's so easy to dissect truths of Scripture from their context and reshape them into new versions of "truth."

Slaves obey your masters; judge not or else you'll be judged; wives submit to your husbands; an eye for an eye and a tooth for a tooth—all familiar concepts that have their origin in Scripture. Yet every one of them, when reinterpreted apart from their proper context, is used to justify behavior that's clearly opposed by the true spirit of Scripture, from cover to cover.

The maddening result: Although *The Bible* has inspired many of the finest contributions to human culture, like the universal brotherhood of mankind, the existence of the human soul, and the equality of every individual on this planet, it's also inspired some of the most damaging, such as slavery, genocide, and warfare.

How and why can such contradictory energies be fueled by the same source of inspiration? And more importantly, how is this paradoxical nature of Scripture exploited by the enemies of truth who seek to confound our understanding of it at every turn?

These questions are precisely what this book, *Fish Tales (From the Belly of the Whale)*, will seek to answer, so that by better understanding the numerous factors that contribute to this dilemma, we'll be that much closer to disarming their effect in our lives.

Counting down one misconception after the other, we'll analyze how these biblical concepts have become so misconstrued over time, revealing the three-step principle involved in this process.

Step One: To create a great misconception, latch onto any idea that forms a legitimate basis of biblical truth. Step Two: Isolate that truth from its context and then discourage any reference to other verses that might contradict it. Step Three: Repeat this new version of the so-called "truth," in zealous opposition to all that's contained in the initial version of said truth.

While this process might seem at first too simple to be of any real effectiveness, any doubt as to its power is eliminated upon seeing this three-step principle in action.

For example, if you ask a hundred people, you'll find that practically everyone believes *The Bible* says, "Money is the root of all evil." Here we have a classic case of a great misconception. That's because, one, it presents us with a solid slice of scripturally-based truth; two, it's examined entirely in isolation from its original context; and, three, it's quoted so often and with such conviction that it's actually entered the lexicon of human ideology.

Such simple steps, yes; but consider how effective these three simple steps are, after all. Consider how often you, too, have been tempted to believe that money is the root of all evil—that is, if you consider yourself a true believer of *The Bible*.

Of course you'd only be tempted to believe it should you resist the urge to check Scripture for yourself, because then you'd discover the Apostle Paul really said that the "*love of*" money is the root of all evil, and not as most people assume, that money, in and of itself, is the offending root.

So, if you've ever wanted to know why *The Bible* presents such a contradictory reality, then it's time to take your own plunge into the belly of the whale. There, you'll discover that just because the sacred truths of Scripture have often been distorted by those who wish to turn light into darkness, this isn't the final chapter of the tale. And in the end, you'll find that when God sets forth His intention in Scripture, He actually means what He says and says what He means, regardless of centuries of disinformation that contribute to the greatest misconceptions ever blamed on *The Bible*.

Concepts in Misconceptions

THE BIBLE is undoubtedly the most influential book of all time. To many, it's a wellspring of divine wisdom; to others, the source of insidious disinformation. It inspires mankind with the deepest solemnities, and it conjures up the darkest horrors. It stimulates the sublime, and justifies the perverse.

Much of the world's greatest literature and art springs—like Athena, fully grown—from Scripture: Dante's *Divine Comedy*, Blake's *Marriage of Heaven and Hell*, Rembrandt's *Belshazzar's Feast*, Michelangelo's *David*, and DeMille's *The Ten Commandments*. It's profoundly impacted philosophy, science, technology, and politics: Newton's *Mathematical Principles of Natural Philosophy*, Kepler's *Laws of Planetary Motion*, da Vinci's *Codex on the Flight of Birds*, and Jefferson's *Declaration of the Causes and Necessity of Taking Up Arms*.

But unfortunately, *The Bible* has also been used as a force for evil in the world, as many individuals, institutions, and movements have twisted its truths to serve their own purposes. Through a subtle manipulation of its message, Scripture has been used to justify the enslavement of humans, the subjection of women, and the slaughter of the animal kingdom. As the inspiration for social engineering, it's produced such ill-fated ventures as Utopianism and Socialism, and such dastardly movements as the Salem Witch Hunts and the Spanish Inquisition. Manifested into a social system, it's been used to underpin inhumane political regimes like Fascism, Nazism, and Communism.

In light of such historical evidence, it's clear that no one is immune from *The Bible*'s ability to both bless and curse anyone who encounters its strangely contradictory contents. When one expects to find a basis for hope and peace in Scripture, we find instead the seeds of despair and strife. Instead of illuminating our hearts with light and truth, it imparts darkness and confusion.

Just think how often in your own experience you've been confronted with some apparently profound gem of wisdom, only to find yourself wondering why it just doesn't seem to ring true. You ask yourself about the source of this so-called "gem." So you search your heart, you search every book you can find on the subject, and more importantly, you search the Scriptures, hoping to discover the origin of this gem. Yet much to your chagrin, you find you've fallen short of your goal. Nowhere is that particular truth expressed the way it was told to you. Why, you ask, should this be the case?

Sadly, it's because in many instances the so-called "truths" we're being sold are nothing more than a bill of goods, a mere shadow of the original facts. They're "truths" that have been watered down, regurgitated, and repackaged under a different frame of reference from the one in which they were first conceived. Worse still, when you search *The Bible* from cover to cover, you find that the verse as it was quoted to you is conspicuously absent, as is anything even remotely resembling it. So you're left more confused than ever and haunted by the thought that there's no point in searching any longer because there's no real basis for truth in the first place.

Yet, like a thirsty pilgrim, you cling to the hope that eventually you'll stumble onto the spring of truth. And you do so because that's the way God made us. Built into our very nature is a yearning for the truth, a hunger that by God's design can't be stifled, no matter how much the world, the flesh, and the devil conspire to dull it. As the great Christian apologetic C.S. Lewis pointed out:

> We're like people who must believe in the reality of Heaven even though we've yet to go there ourselves, even as people who may have never tasted food or water would still know that such things as food and water existed simply because we're men and women who hunger and thirst for them.

In other words, even if we'd never seen or tasted food or water, we'd at least know of their existence because of our desire for them. As such, we could never resist the urge to find food and water, no matter how hard we tried to live without them.

Likewise, we must persevere in trying to discover the true meaning of what our hearts and minds grapple with daily. We must continue striving to understand the true nature of reality, because otherwise we're robbed of our most valuable quality, which is our desire to seek truth and grasp at it, regardless of what others may think of our homely efforts. We do so because something deep down inside us can and does comprehend the truth when we see or hear it, in spite of all our doubts and fears to the contrary.

This ability to instinctually recognize the truth is, in fact, the essence of what it means to be human. In this, we catch a glimpse into one of the most sublime paradoxes mankind has yet to contemplate, as Albert Einstein explained: "The great mystery of the Universe is ... its comprehensibility."

That said, how do we go about rescuing the truth from these centuries-old incursions? How do we strip away so many layers of disinformation? Our first order of business, I believe, is to consider how biblical misconceptions get started in the first place. Like most fallacies that humans insist on embracing, a great misconception is always based on a foundation of genuine truth. The more closely an idea seems to originate from a legitimate basis, then all the better, no matter how absurd or outrageous that idea appears.

Such is the case with the familiar adage: "Once in grace, always in grace." It doesn't matter that it's not in *The Bible*. People assume it's there because it sounds scriptural. That's because, in principle, it is based on real biblical wisdom. The only problem: The principle speaks of God's integrity and faithfulness, and not—I repeat, *not*—of those who are trying to connect with Him because He can be trusted.

Unfortunately, the idea that once you've entered into a relationship with God you're locked into a perpetual relationship with Him, no matter what you do thereafter, simply has no scriptural foundation. To this very point *The Book of Hebrews* is quite emphatic, from first to last. According to it, you stay in God's grace if, and only if, you continue in the way you began.[4] You begin your relationship with God by having faith, and therefore you must continue the trip, right up until the end, with the same kind of faith that got you started.

Otherwise you end up like those miserable Israelites, who began their wilderness journey in faith, having witnessed God's deliverance at every turn, only to find themselves wandering in a circle for four long decades, just a few miles short of the Promised Land.[5]

So, apart from having to get over the shock that this verse isn't in *The Bible*, the next question is: How does one tell the difference, logically and honestly, between the original truth and its counterfeit?

The answer: In spite of all the forces that obscure the truth, the forms of disinformation still persist in revealing conspicuous patterns, so that upon further inspection of these patterns, a higher truth emerges which enables us to discern the original from the counterfeit.

To demonstrate this, let's consider the next aspect of a great misconception. Take an actual truth found in *The Bible*, and isolate it from its context. Again, the more subtle that this process of isolation is executed, all the better. In this way, almost any manner of disinformation can be blamed on *The Bible*.

A classic example of this technique involves a famous passage in the twenty-fourth chapter of *The Gospel of Matthew* where Jesus' disciples asked Him when the End of the Age would occur. As tradition would have us believe, Jesus told them that not even He knew when it would occur, that only His Father in Heaven knew the day or

---

[4] *Hebrews* 3:14

[5] Ibid. 3:8-19

the hour. But if you examine the context of His conversation, you might be surprised to find out that Jesus really said:

> Heaven and Earth will pass away, but My words will never pass away. No man knows about *that* day or hour, not the angels in Heaven, or the Son, but only the Father.[6]

From this, we see that Jesus was talking about the day when Heaven and Earth will pass away, and not His Second Coming, which as anyone who's studied *The Bible* knows will be followed by the long-awaited Millennial Reign. Then, after the Millennium, Satan, who's bound for the duration of this thousand-year period, will be loosed for "a little season," after which he leads one final rebellion against God and is then thrown into the Lake of Fire.[7]

By allowing the context of this statement to convey its meaning, we're able to determine what day and hour Jesus was really talking about. He was describing an event that occurs at a different moment in the biblical timeline—after the Second Coming, after the Millennium, after the "little season," after Satan is thrown into the Lake of Fire, and after the Final Judgment.

Following all of these events, then, the twenty-first chapter of *The Book of Revelation* opens with the words:

> And I saw a new Heaven and a new Earth, because the first Heaven and first Earth had *passed away*, and the sea was no more.[8]

Another persistent pattern of the great misconceptions of *The Bible* is to take a truth found in Scripture and, through a sustained campaign of manipulation, create a new version that eventually becomes synonymous with the original truth, thereby replacing it in the memory traces of humanity.

For example, there's the case of probably the most familiar verse ever to be blamed on *The Bible*. In its original form, it reads as the Apostle Paul warning Timothy that "the love of money is the root of all evil."[9] But so many centuries of distortion have woven such an impenetrable blanket of tradition over this passage that everyone is now convinced that Paul said, "*Money* is the root of all evil." Such a huge shift in meaning, and all accomplished through the omission of just three little words: "…*the love of.*"

---

[6] *Matthew* 24:35-36

[7] *Revelation* 20:1-10

[8] Ibid. 21:1

[9] *First Timothy* 6:10

Likewise, *The Bible* contains the well-known prohibition in the form of the Sixth Commandment. In it, we read: "You should not kill." As a result, generation after generation have read this verse as condemning any form of killing, no matter how justified it might seem in human terms. Usually one hears this verse being intoned in the context of self-defense or police protection.

But anyone who takes the time to read this passage in the original Hebrew language will discover that it actually reads: "You should not *murder*." Naturally, this interpretation dramatically shifts the meaning of this passage, thereby easing the conscience of many a dutiful soldier or police officer.

By correctly translating such words, we're also able to understand events which have long plagued readers of *The Old Testament*, who find themselves confused by a God Who apparently has no problem with sending the Israelites into battle after battle, in the much-understood Conquest of Canaan.

So there you have it. You've seen just how to create a great misconception of *The Bible*. Understand this subtle yet powerful process, and you'll be better prepared to reverse its effect in your own life. Let's review.

Step One: Latch onto a truth that seems to be so thoroughly based on Scripture that upon hearing it your audience is convinced it's in there, as in: "Once in grace, always in grace." Never mind that you can't find it in *The Bible*. So what; it sounds like it is, right?

Step Two: Isolate a known passage from its context so that ever after no one suspects there might be an alternative meaning of those words, like when Jesus said, "No one knows the day or the hour, not even Me." Who cares if this passage isn't referring to the event that tradition claims it does, as long as everyone agrees that it is.

And finally, Step Three: Repeat this new version of the "truth," until eventually whatever truth was once obvious is rendered altogether alien from its initial reality, as with the supposed verses: "Money is the root of all evil" or "You should not kill."

In this way, even a solid mountain of truth can be whittled away until there's nothing left but a dusty pile of clichés. Thus, what Jesus said has never been truer:

> You reject the commands of God so you can keep your own vain traditions, but by persisting on teaching such nonsense, you simply make God's word useless to you.[10]

---

[10] *Mark* 7:9, 13

From the Least to the Greatest

NONE OF THE following essays are intended to say all that can be said on the subjects addressed here. They're merely "ice-breakers," if you will, designed to begin reversing the ages-long atrophy that has stymied a *Bible*-oriented view of them. In doing so, I hope to begin a new chapter in their ongoing history.

As for the order in which they appear, I assure you a great deal of thought has gone into their arrangement. Numerous factors have been considered, particularly the way that certain misconceptions have inspired the most harm to the largest segment of humanity for which the God of *The Bible* undoubtedly intended a far kinder fate. However, because the accuracy of which ones should be considered the greatest misconceptions is a matter of personal conscience, I don't claim their order is verifiable according to any divine principle of understanding on my part.

Another important factor is how the order of the list itself helps to illuminate the main argument of this work, which is to answer the question of how these misconceptions came into being in the first place. Because of this, it must be noted that should the reader skip ahead to those misconceptions that interest only them and so, "rearrange their order," as it were, an understanding of their content will be altered. In short, the order of the list, though not set in stone, does contain a logical flow in which the reading of one essay will lend itself to a better understanding of the one that follows, and so on and so forth.

That said, I can assure the reader that all due diligence has been exhausted in trying to provide a logic to their unfolding, from the least of the fifty misconceptions to the greatest. Therefore, in addition to ordering the list in terms of their social impact and the way this order affects its reception, the next factor that was considered was the degree to which certain ideas have become "synonymous" with *The Bible* as opposed to their being merely "endorsed" by it.

By that I mean that many of the misconceptions on the list, like the Israelites always being slaves in Egypt prior to the Exodus, or God sending serpents after them once they began their wilderness journey, clearly originate from *The Bible*. But because they've never been seen as more than incidental stories, they can be easily neutralized by pointing out the scriptural context in which they've been written. Granted, such tall tales are maddening, particularly because of the way they undermine an appreciation for the integrity of God's word. But they're still not as dangerous as those that have moved beyond the status of mere anecdote and taken on the aura of Scripture itself, such as "Money is the root of evil," or "You should not kill," or "Once in grace, always in grace." The misconceptions that fall into this latter category, due to their having insinuated themselves into the very fabric of Scripture, are much more difficult to counteract; and for that reason alone, they find themselves nearer to the top of our list.

But first, it's time to lay a foundation for verifying the soundness of such decisions, time now to proceed to the first portion of our list en route to that greatest of all misconceptions ever to be blamed on *The Bible*.

REEL ONE

The Hook
#50-34

Misconception #50

Before the Tower of Babel, Everyone Spoke Just One Language

THE FIRST BOOK of *The Bible* tells us of an ancient world in which all humanity spoke a single language. Then, at some point, the people united to thwart God's purposes and, as a result, were punished for their rebellion by being scattered. This scattering was done, according to *The Book of Genesis*, through a miraculous event known as the "Confusion of Tongues," whereby God simultaneously rendered all humans incapable of understanding the language of any family but their own.

Naturally, this story has many implications. Interpreted as an origin myth, scholars have assumed it's simply a quaint tale designed to explain the inexplicable—of how all the different languages of humanity began. As such, this story seems to provide a neat and concise—however far-fetched—answer in our pursuit to understand the origins of human culture.

In the case of this present study, though, we're not just trying to understand the foibles of human language; we're trying to determine if *The Bible* can be accepted as a valid record of history and not just a series of naïve traditions conceived by so many misguided primitives. And to do this, we require more than stories like this to explain our origins; we need to know if *The Bible* has the ability to say what it means and mean what it says. Then and only then are we capable of having what *The Bible* calls "faith." And when I say that, I don't mean having faith in tales of magical worlds and mysterious acts of sorcery. I'm talking about having faith in a world that God alone can order for the sake of a humanity that can perceive that world in all its sublime wonder.

With that in mind, let's examine what *The Bible* has to say about this phase of human development and how centuries of tradition have altered the scriptural context in which this story sprang.

The eleventh chapter of *Genesis* records:

> And the whole Earth was speaking one language, and it came to pass, as they journeyed from the east, that they found a plain in the land of Shinar, and they dwelt there. And they

said to one another, "Let's build a city and a tower whose top will reach Heaven, and let's make a name for ourselves, or else we'll be scattered."

And the Lord said, "Look, the people are united, and they all have one language, and now nothing will be restrained from them which they've imagined to do. Therefore, let's go down and confuse their language so they'll no longer be able to understand one another."

So the Lord scattered them across the face of the Earth, and they stopped building their city. And that's why the name of that city is called Babel, because there the Lord confused the language of the whole world.[11]

So there you have it—an origin story that provides us with a concise explanation, however fantastic, of how humans evolved from a single language root into a multi-branched tree of languages. Pretty straightforward stuff, right? I mean, thousands of years of tradition must be accurate about what *The Bible* says, wouldn't you agree?

But wait; not so fast. Don't forget our three laws of disinformation! First, latch onto a genuine truth of Scripture. Second, isolate that truth from its context. And third, repeat the new version of the "truth" until it's rendered altogether alien from its original meaning.

Now, let's see how this process has affected this familiar *Bible* story. First, place the story, depicted in the eleventh chapter of *Genesis*, on a pedestal of boundless conviction. Then, excise it from the rest of the book to create the impression that Scripture has nothing else to say about it. And finally, repeat this version of the story, again and again, thereby removing any doubt that *The Bible* or any of its supporters are anything but in complete agreement with this revised version.

The end result: From the beginning of time, mankind always spoke in a single language until they attempted to unite in an unholy alliance to undermine heavenly authority. Then God got fed up and, to subvert their power grab, He divided their language into many different ones, thereby scattering their efforts to the wind. The End, right?

Again I say: Not so fast!

Still, I can sense an argument from many people. You may be asking: "But won't I be rejecting *The Bible* if I no longer believe this story the way it's been told all these years?"

Fortunately, the answer is: "No, you won't be rejecting *The Bible* if you simply allow it to fill in the missing pieces of the puzzle on its own."

---

[11] *Genesis* 11:1-9

Never mind about human traditions that have only managed to provide us with an incomplete picture of this story, because as it turns out, *The Bible* really does have more to say on this subject than we've been led to believe. What's more, it's imperative that we come to a fuller understanding of what it says about this subject because so many people's faith are depending on a genuine awareness of what the Scriptures really say, and not merely a half-baked version of them.

I mean, if *The Bible* supposedly reports on important events in humanity's history, then shouldn't it be allowed to speak for itself? In the end, it'll prove its own ability to validate itself. If not, then the skeptics and naysayers will forever think themselves capable of toppling the truth of Scripture. Therefore, it's always our job as truth seekers to dig to the bottom of every mystery, no matter how much it may rattle our own cherished traditions.

And to think: The antidote for this kind of disinformation is simply a willingness to read *The Bible* for oneself. Stranger still, we only have to read the chapter immediately preceding the eleventh chapter of *Genesis*. Let's see for ourselves:

> Now these are the generations of the sons of Noah: They are Shem, Ham, and Japheth, and to them were born sons after the Great Flood. The sons of Japheth were Gomer, Magog, Madai, Javan, Tubal, Meshech, and Tiras. By these were the isles of the Gentiles divided in their lands; every one of them *after their own tongue*, after their families, and in their nations. And the sons of Ham were Cush, Mizraim, Phut, and Canaan. These are the sons of Ham, *after their tongues*, in their countries, and in their nations. And to Shem, the father of all the children of Eber, the brother of Japheth, the oldest, even to him were born children, including Elam, Asshur, Arphaxad, Lud, and Aram. So these are the sons of Shem, after their families, *after their tongues*, in their lands, and after their nations.[12]

Imagine that: In a plain and simple way, *The Bible* itself defies the misconception that before the Flood everyone spoke just one language. The tenth chapter of *Genesis* depicts a world where, before the Tower of Babel was ever conceived, the sons of Noah already spoke separate languages, each according to their own nation, country, and family, much as in today's world where geographical divides cause a language to splinter into a multiplicity of dialects.

In light of this context, then, we might better understand the hidden meaning in that simple phrase in *Genesis* that we've already

---

[12] *Genesis* 10:1-31

visited but that can now be seen differently. Let's review that phrase.

> And the Lord said, "Look, the people are united, and they all have one language, and now nothing will be restrained from them which they've imagined to do."[13]

Now that we've allowed Scripture itself to provide the much-needed context for this statement, the picture that emerges is one of a multilingual culture that existed before Nimrod's rule. Under the sway of Nimrod, however, a once-diverse people were assimilated into a homogeneous group, and all facilitated by this trend toward speaking a single language. It was this shift from multiple languages, then, to a single language that set the stage for a worldwide rebellion against God, as indicated by the words: "The people are united; they all have one language, and *now* nothing will restrain them."

So, as it turns out, it was Nimrod's homogenizing process, where everyone spoke the same language, that was at the heart of this rebellion, and which was undoubtedly why God struck at this aspect of it. In short, if a unification of language turned humanity into a virtually unstoppable mob, then a restoration of that diversity was all that was needed to quell such a rebellion; hence, the Confusion of Tongues.

With this new view in sight, the only question that remains is: If *The Bible* itself never insisted that mankind always spoke a single language before the Tower of Babel, then why would tradition have been so persistent as to this rendition of history?

The answer, I believe, lies in the frame of reference that became prevalent in the Age of Enlightenment, when mankind came to embrace reason and rationality in favor of revelation and spirituality. More importantly, in terms of this study of the processes of disinformation, it should be noted this shift in our worldview didn't occur overnight. It was the by-product of centuries of abuse that grew out of an overemphasis on revelation knowledge, in which modern man became suspicious—and rightly so, though I disagree with the end result of such pessimism—of a privileged few who claimed to have a corner on wisdom at the expense of the uninitiated.

In rejecting the notion of divine intervention, modern thinkers began to view the history of knowledge as an exclusively human enterprise. From this, the idea sprang up that societies underwent periodic transformations that evolved from a lower, primitive state to a higher, civilized state. In turn, this view of the incremental progression of human culture was overlaid onto the societies that were

---

[13] *Genesis* 11:6

depicted in the biblical record as well. Accordingly, the first families and nations depicted there would've been seen as being incapable of anything but the most primitive modes of thought.

As such, a story about the origins of human language would've suffered from this same *a priori* position. Therefore, anything in *The Bible* that even hinted at this now-familiar pattern—from simple to complex, from single to many—would've been assumed to be the correct one. Thus, the story of the Tower of Babel, in which the earliest families of humanity seemed to all be speaking a single language from the start, provided a perfect synthesis between science and theology. Too nice a fit, in fact, for anyone to dare disagree that it might not actually be true, even though it requires a total disregard for the *Genesis* record as a whole, which, upon further review, clearly contradicts this cherished paradigm.

Misconception #49

All the Curses Inflicted by God are Perpetual in Nature

ONE OF THE most confusing things we humans face when considering God's personality is the way *The Bible* describes Him as being both a God of infinite love and a God of unquenchable anger. A consuming, dreadful fire, on one hand, and a calming, gentle breeze, on the other. It's this double-edged nature of God that more than anything else stabs at our confused minds. Exactly how can a supposedly loving God not only pronounce blessings of hope upon humanity but pronounce curses of doom on them as well?

It'd be so easy to simply shrug one's shoulders and write it off as just another of those impenetrable mysteries of God that no one dare question. But unfortunately, by avoiding this issue, we end up overlooking a very important aspect of God's personality. Therefore, we'll do our best to address this issue, if only for the sake of trying to scratch the surface regarding this much-misunderstood subject.

The starting point in trying to understand this side of God's personality is to first examine our own heart—spiritually speaking, that is—because it's actually an extension of the divine nature that God placed in all of us. As such, our emotions and reactions run the gamut of human experience; we love and we hate, we nurture and we destroy, we bless and we curse. So why wouldn't we expect the God Who made us to do the same thing, even if what He does is by nature on a much grander scale?

With that in mind, let's look at one of the most well-known curses of God in Scripture.

According to tradition, *The Book of Genesis* records the time when God confronted Eve for eating the Fruit of the Tree of Knowledge, whereupon He pronounced a curse that impacted not just her but every one of Eve's female descendants.

> To the woman God said, "I'll intensify your sorrow, even to the point of your giving birth in pain so through suffering you'll bring forth your children. Not only that, but your desire will no longer be satisfied through your own bidding, but

you'll be controlled by your husband, and from now on he will dominate you."[14]

Ever since that fateful day, the history of the world, like a great mirror held up to confirm or deny the truth of God's word, has borne witness to all of it. Ever since, women really have endured the pain of childbirth, the struggle for personal freedom, and the domination of men in every area of their lives. All of it testifying to the genuineness of that primordial prophecy.

Considering the apparent effectiveness of such a curse, the only question that remains is: Was this curse ever intended to be perpetual in nature? In other words, once God uttered it, was it supposed to be a curse without restriction, without end?

Well, based on the attitude of those who claim to believe in Scripture, you'd certainly think so, wouldn't you? Think of how many *Bible*-believing men love to quote this verse just when they find themselves losing an argument with an intelligent, strong-willed woman. That's when they suddenly feel it's their heavenly duty to make sure that no woman ever gets one over on one of God's divinely-inspired men.

Then, having successfully completed "stage one" of every good disinformation strategy, they just as quickly move on to "stage two" by isolating this verse from any others in Scripture that extol the overwhelmingly positive impact women have had throughout biblical history.

And moving on to "stage three," they repeat this well-worn verse so often and so passionately that even God Himself is sometimes tempted to believe that half of His creation is superior to the other half. Never mind that when we ask the husband where his wife is, we refer to her as his "better half." Just ignore annoying, anecdotal details like that, and keep repeating the story the way it's always been told, and before you know it, you, too, will discover just how effective this method is in lording it over any woman of your choice.

So, there you have it: Another perfectly orchestrated attack on the truth as it's recorded in *The Bible*.

But, returning to our earlier question: Is that all there is to the story of Eve's curse? Yes, the historical record testifies that God meant what He said; yes, men have done their damnedest to make it stick—howbeit doing so while in a self-induced state of amnesia concerning those curses in *Genesis* that pertain to them. Nevertheless, does any of the foregoing prove that God intended for this curse of Eve to last forever?

---

[14] *Genesis* 3:16

After all, everyone has a stake in answering this question, not just Eve and her daughters, because if they're forever cursed, then that also means Adam and his sons are, too. So keep in mind, when we seek to answer this question concerning Eve, there's much more at stake than some of us might first have imagined.

So, what does *The Bible* have to say about the curses that God has pronounced upon His creatures? Is there really nothing more than perpetual doom for every recipient of His wrath? Let's take time, then, to search out what else the Scriptures say about this very perplexing subject.

Actually, the verse in *Genesis* immediately preceding the curse of Eve supplies us with the antidote that we're seeking. In it, *The Bible* records the curse that God uttered against the serpent who was, after all, the true instigator in this whole tragic affair.

> And the Lord said to the serpent, "Because you've done this thing, you'll be cursed beyond all animals, and as a result, you'll crawl around on your belly, eating dust your entire life. And I'll create hostility between you and the woman, between your children and her children; and it'll crush your head, and you'll bruise his heel."[15]

According to most theologians, this verse actually contains the primordial kernel of every biblical prophecy that will ever unfold up to the end of time. And considering its ambiguous nature, it's very important that we take some time to break down its meaning.

All biblical scholars believe that, even though God seems to be cursing the serpent who deceived Adam and Eve, He's really talking to Satan. Addressing the creature that motivated the serpent in the first place, God tells the devil that He'll create hostility between him and humanity, and because of this hostility, a war will ensue between the devil's children and Eve's children. But in the end, it's going to be a child of Eve, which is to say, Christ Jesus, Who'll destroy the power of Satan.

Understood in that context, the same verse in *Genesis* could read:

> And the Lord said to the serpent: "Because you've done this thing (in conspiring to trick Eve), you'll be cursed beyond all animals, and as a result you'll crawl around on your belly, eating dust your entire life. And I'll create hostility between you (speaking of Satan, who was really behind the actions of the serpent) and the (descendants of the) woman, between

---

[15] *Genesis* 3:14-15

your children (of the devil) and her children (of humanity); and it's this child (of Eve's, which is to say, Christ) Who will crush your head (which speaks of Satan's power), and you (the devil) will bruise His heel (that is to say, the human component of the Messiah)."

Tying all this together, we can deduce that when Jesus was nailed to the tree of Golgotha, it was to fulfill this prophecy in *Genesis*. As the Apostle Paul later described it:

Christ has redeemed us from the curse of the Law, having been made a curse for our sakes, because it is written: "Anyone who hangs on a tree is cursed!"
In this way, the blessing of Abraham is able to come upon the Gentiles because of what Jesus Christ has done so that we might receive the promise of God's Spirit through our faith.[16]

Once again, we can thank God for His written word when it comes to defending ourselves against those who'd hunt and peck us to death with their limited view of what *The Bible* supposedly says. In other words, without reconciling the paradox of God's written record with humanity's historical record, we might as well tell a woman living in today's world that when she goes into labor, she should bravely cope with the pain without the aid of modern medicine. Tell her God wants her to suffer the pains of childbirth because it's His perfect will for her to endure the pain, just as Eve was forced to endure the pain. Then tell her it'll always be God's desire for her to suffer the pain of childbirth, because He was the One Who instigated this curse in the first place. Pretty absurd, don't you think?

Of course it is; which is to say, it is, according to an appropriate understanding of God's word, in relationship to the Advent of Christ, which states:

Christ suffered for us, having left us an example so that we should follow in His footsteps...
When He suffered, He never threatened anyone in return, but He committed Himself to the One Who judges righteously and bore our sins in His own body on that tree so that we, being dead to our sins, should live for the sake of righteousness, by whose stripes we were healed.[17]

---

[16] *Galatians* 3:13-14

[17] *First Peter* 2:21-24

In light of these facts, then, why would anyone believe that all the curses of God are perpetual in nature?

One reason is because most people suffer from a shortsighted view of Scripture. The tendency is always to focus on just one aspect of *The Bible* while de-emphasizing the rest of the story. So, because the deepest truths of Scripture are paradoxical in nature, it's virtually impossible to grasp the totality of God's word using this approach.

Consequently, people start evaluating God's personality in terms of their own limited view of Scripture. Human pet peeves then become God's supposed pet peeves; human interpretations of the human condition become God's supposed view of the human condition, and so on. In this, it's just as Jesus warned us about so long ago: "The traditions of mankind invariably nullify the word of God."

What happens next?

Not surprisingly, you eventually have a world running rampant with skeptics and critics. Skeptics love to deny that God curses or blesses anyone for any reason; critics seek to downplay the idea that the death and resurrection of Christ ushered in a new era of grace and peace.

But no matter. Regardless of all the naysaying of skeptics and critics, Christ accomplished something on Calvary that allowed God to lift His curse from anyone who'd simply trust Him. And for that, we who've received the gift of God's grace and peace in that act of trust will forever be grateful—men *and women* alike.

Misconception #48

*When the Disciples Asked Jesus When He'd
Establish His Kingdom, He Said They'd
Have to Wait Till the End of the Age*

THE DISCIPLES of Jesus nervously huddled about their self-assured leader as they quizzed Him about their uncertain future. Brutally oppressed by their Roman overlords, the disciples were anxious for Jesus to tell them something that would give them hope in a world where all hope seemed lost: "Lord, when will the glorious promises of our God finally deliver us from oppression and set us free?" "How much longer, Jesus, will You wander about as a mere itinerant preacher while we wait so patiently?" "And with our lives hanging in the balance every moment, what is taking You so long to manifest Your power?"

To which Jesus casually replied: "I'm afraid that, My friends, is something that will simply have to wait till the End of the Age; until then you're just going to have to grin and bear it like good little soldiers in the cause."

So a disciple asked, "Well, if that's the case, then can You at least tell us what the signs of Your Second Coming will be? What should we look for as the End of the World approaches?"

Jesus then began His famous discourse about His reappearance in the Last Days, much to the dismay, I'm sure, of everyone there who were all hoping for at least a ray of hope in their own lifetime.

So goes the story—at least, as it's told and retold in most churches to this day.

But is that really the whole truth, and nothing but the truth, so help us God? Certainly, Jesus couldn't have been so indifferent to the suffering of the very people He was about to sacrifice His life for. So what gives? Let's take a moment to discuss what seems to be lacking.

The real culprit in this scenario lies in the fact that we're dealing with a translation problem. In this case, the passage in *Matthew* fails to convey its total meaning because the Greek word used to describe the word for "coming," as in the Coming of the Lord, is *parousia*, which can just as easily be translated "presence." Said Matthew:

And Jesus left the Temple and was going His way, when the disciples came to look at the buildings there. But Jesus said to them, "Do you see this place? I tell you with all certainty that not one stone here will be left standing; it'll all come crashing down someday."

And as He sat upon the Mount of Olives, the disciples came to Him privately, and said, "Please tell us when this will occur; and what will be the sign of Your Coming (*parousia*), and the End of the Age?"[18]

Then later in the same chapter, we find that Jesus said:

For as the lightning comes out of the east, and shines even to the west, so also the Coming (*parousia*) of the Son of Man will be.[19]

And still later:

But as it was in the days of Noah, so also the Coming (*parousia*) of the Son of Man will be... The people at that time had no idea what was going to happen to them until finally the Flood came and swept them all away; so likewise the Coming (*parousia*) of the Son of Man will be.[20]

In every instance, then, what Jesus said to His disciples was far beyond what they were capable of understanding at the time. They equated the "Coming" of Christ with the event Jesus described as the "someday" when the Temple was going to be destroyed. In hindsight, however, we can now see this wasn't the case in the mind of Jesus, Who understood what humanity would only realize after a great deal more history rolled on to fill in the hidden meaning of His words.

Only in hindsight can we now see that Jesus wasn't describing a future coming, as the disciples had assumed. He was describing the advent of His abiding "presence," which had already occurred in their midst, even though the disciples would require much more time and experience to fully grasp what that meant.

Only by allowing for this alternate interpretation of the Greek word, *parousia*, can we now rethink our previous view of Jesus' response to His disciples and see the answer He gave them in an entirely new light.

Because of the dire nature of their circumstances, the disciples

---

[18] *Matthew* 24:1-3

[19] Ibid. 24:27

[20] Ibid. 24:37, 39

would have found it very difficult to grasp the logic of a deliverance that was too far off in the distant future to do them any good. And doubtlessly, Jesus would've understood this. To say otherwise would be absurd. But tradition is a tough thing to shake. All that most people focus on is that when the anxious disciples pressed Jesus to "send in the cavalry" to rescue them, He proceeded to blow their minds by telling them about future events, such as wars and rumors of wars, famines, pestilences, earthquakes, and false prophets.

In the face of such bewildering predictions, it's easy to imagine the disappointment that the disciples must have felt.

But, as we're beginning to see in our analysis of the laws of disinformation, any pessimism about the events predicted for the End of the Age must be understood in terms of our own natural tendency to isolate most biblical texts from the context in which they actually exist. Seen in isolation, the gloomier predictions in these famous passages are usually assumed to be the only ones found there. Thus, those who think Jesus never offered His disciples anything but gloom and doom, do so only because they ignore the rest of what He said about the promise of His "presence."

It's true: Trials and tribulations are the lot of anyone who dares to follow Christ. But it's just as true that "anyone who endures to the end will be rescued,"[21] and that, en route to that rescue, "where sin abounds, grace abounds much more."[22]

So, when we re-examine the situation in its totality, we see that Jesus' intention was never to disappoint His disciples with the bad news that He was forestalling their salvation until some future time. Instead, like the Good Shepherd that He was, He was telling them about the reality of His *parousia*, His abiding "presence." Because even though His present work couldn't be completed in their lifetimes, and much would have to wait until such time as had been determined, nothing could prevent His *parousia* from accomplishing great things for them, then and there, even in the midst of their current predicament.

At first, this may be difficult to comprehend, but try to think of it in the following terms.

Since God's first promise in *The Old Testament* to send a Savior to His people, there have been many aspects relating to the nature of this Coming One. Eventually, the body of literature that grew up around this tradition was such that it sometimes was in danger of getting lost in translation. Expectations, hopes, and fears all added to the difficulty of ferreting out what God intended us to know about this Person we

---

[21] *Matthew* 24:13

[22] *Romans* 5:20

were to expect. Centuries of tradition pit one interpretation of a biblical passage over against another. Texts were removed from their context. Distortions were repeated. But of course all of this is to be expected, right? It's just the three laws of disinformation at work, naturally. No problem; the Lord of the Word knows how to provide a solution to cut through all the clutter.

Because God understands the tricky nature of disseminating the truth via the written word, He deigned to send numerous deliverers, messiahs, and saviors to facilitate the process. Beginning with such luminaries as Enoch, Noah, and Abraham, God raised up many great men in preparation for the eventual arrival of the One Who was to come. We know this because of early prophecies regarding a deliverer contained in extra-biblical texts like *The Book of Jasher*, also known as *The Upright Record*. According to scholars like Cyrus H. Gordon, *Jasher* was a literary source from which biblical authors borrowed to write their books. Proof of this, they say, is the way *The Old Testament* quotes from *Jasher* twice: First, in *Joshua* 10:13, and then in *Second Samuel* 1:18. Certainly anyone familiar with Scripture has heard the story of how God helped the Israelites in their battle with the Amorites. In the midst of the conflict, Joshua prayed:

> 'Oh, Sun, stand still over Gibeon, oh, Moon, over the Valley of Aijalon.' So the Sun stood still and the Moon stopped, till the nation avenged itself on its enemies, as it is written in *The Book of Jasher*.[23]

As it so happens, in *Jasher*, we find a prophecy that would have been impossible for the people of that day to distinguish whom the prophet was referring to. Even when we read it today, this prophecy can easily be understood as describing the coming of Jesus, Who was to be *the* Messiah. But as it turns out, this prophecy actually was predicting the life and mission of Moses, who was *a* messianic figure. Only through the hindsight of history, then, would mankind eventually come to a genuine realization of whom God had been speaking about in His drama of prophecy.

The disciples of Jesus fell victim to this same phenomenon. To a man they expected that all the prophecies of the Savior they'd read about their whole lives would be fulfilled in a single, glorious arrival. Promises of blessing and promises of judgment were assumed to be all rolled out into one divine lump. Only over a gradual period of time would they—and us—begin to absorb Jesus' explanations that God's plan of the ages was an unfolding plan. It was never God's intention to

---

[23] *Joshua* 10:12-13

execute His rescue effort in a single, blinding moment but, rather, was to proceed through a series of connected events, each one coming after the other, like wave upon wave rolling onto the seashore.

So, having examined some of the ways the meaning of God's word becomes obscured, let's discuss how *The Bible* helps to provide a counterbalance to the laws of disinformation.

Is there anything else in *The Bible* that could give us a better understanding of God's rescue effort of the human race? Yes, Jesus told His disciples that He was providing them with His abiding "presence." But what good would that do if the Roman Empire continued unabated? Wasn't the Messiah, at His Coming, supposed to destroy the present world order and establish a new one? Yes, the "presence" of God was a marvelous gift. But in light of Jesus' failure to overthrow Roman tyranny, in lieu of some future fulfillment, how could this "presence" of His be seen as anything more than some kind of consolation prize for their heroic discipleship?

Fortunately for us, Matthew wasn't the only gospel writer who recorded the fateful words that Jesus delivered concerning the Coming of the Messiah.

According to Luke, Jesus mentioned something else during this now all-too-familiar discourse. His account records the time leading up to that enigmatic speech, when suddenly the Pharisees interrupted their discussion, demanding that Jesus tell them exactly when the Kingdom of God would be established on Earth.

Calmly, Jesus replied:

> No one will ever notice the arrival of God's kingdom simply by observing some great event. You won't be able to say, "Look, here it is! Or look, there it is!" For you see, the Kingdom of God is within you!

Then, privately, He explained to His disciples:

> The time is approaching when you'll all wish to see the day when the Son of Man arrives, but you won't see it. Many will tell you, "Here it is!" or "There it is!" But don't believe them or follow them, because just as lightning flashes across the whole sky in an instant, so it will also be in that moment when the Son of Man arrives. But before that happens, He must suffer many things.[24]

Now, as it turns out, all of this corresponds much more accurately with the persistent teachings of Christ, who repeatedly explained His

---

[24] *Luke* 17:20-25

views on the nature of God's plan of salvation for humanity. The Kingdom of God, insisted Jesus, was never supposed to be established through force of arms, as Christ's disciples had naïvely and presumptuously anticipated. No, His kingdom wasn't going to be one that waited for some shattering, global intrusion. It would first be established, in its fullness, via the hearts and minds of men and women of faith.

Of course, there'd be many who'd balk at this notion on the grounds that *The Bible* clearly speaks of a future day when Christ, as Conquering Hero, will split the sky and return to set up His kingdom once and for all. But in this rigid application of biblical prophecy, one would actually reveal the extent to which even modern believers are still susceptible to age-old preconceived notions of salvation.

As it was then, so it is today.

In this, we again see how important it is to examine each and every verse within its proper context. Then and only then is it possible to discover for ourselves how tradition—based more upon human expectation and hope than the truth of Scripture—can warp the original meaning of any isolated portion of Scripture.

Unless we read *Matthew* 24, together with *Luke* 17, and mindfully weave their narratives together, it's just as easy to fall victim to the same mind-set as those early followers of Jesus.

So, if *The Bible* has always provided a counterbalance to the lopsided view that Jesus was only speaking about His Second Coming in this famous discourse, why are traditions so persistent in insisting this to be the case?

I believe it's because we humans all share a common weakness: We hear what we expect to hear; and when given a choice between two alternatives, we usually assume the worst. So, when history failed to pan out in favor of the conquering Messiah interpretation of Scripture, even we, in hindsight, assume the worst. History didn't witness the intrusion of Jesus as Triumphant Hero; therefore, He must have failed. Right?

Whether from the view of the disciples, or from ours some two thousand years later, the mission of Jesus seems to be nothing more than a wasted effort, a noble plan that failed to materialize, much akin to those numerous attempts at creating Utopian societies that all eventually collapsed under their own weight.

In light of the proper context, however, provided by a better understanding of Jesus' comments about His abiding "presence," we begin to see things differently. When we accept that Jesus was serious about His kingdom not being an outward, obvious place, but an unseen kingdom established in the hearts of humanity, we're able to reevaluate

Jesus' seemingly lackadaisical response to His disciples. Just because He didn't exhibit the same enthusiasm that they did, in hoping for the immediate downfall of the Roman Empire, didn't mean He was unwilling to do anything about the problem. To say that Jesus wasn't interested in seeing the overthrow of tyranny is as absurd as it is far-fetched. We're not talking about a disagreement in purpose, then; we're talking about a misunderstanding of the method by which Jesus proposed that this purpose would be achieved.

What never even occurred to the disciples, Jesus knew all too well: Why bother expending one's effort in trying to topple an earthly kingdom when God planned to establish His kingdom without the need for political revolution? The fallacy, in looking for the Conquering Messiah, is in assuming the Kingdom of God can't be established until that spectacular moment in history occurs.

Make that mistake, though, invest all your hopes and dreams in that future day of the Conqueror, and you'll find that you've missed the true Advent of Christ. The boat sailed, but you weren't on board; all because you thought you'd wait for something better.

And it set sail in Jesus' day, not *en masse* by the boatload, but one person at time, one act of faith at a time, one implantation of His abiding "presence" at a time.

If this is the true significance of what's revealed in the gospel record of both Matthew and Luke, then we need look no further than Jesus' parables of the kingdom to confirm this subtle yet potent idea, in which He said:

> The Kingdom of Heaven is like that of a grain of mustard, which a man took, and sowed in his field. And even though it's the smallest of all seeds, when it grows up, it's the greatest among all plants, eventually becoming a tree, so that even the birds are able to lodge in its branches.

And again in another parable, Jesus said:

> The Kingdom of Heaven is like a lump of leaven, which a woman took, and hid in three measures of meal, until finally the whole lump was leavened.[25]

---

[25] *Matthew* 13:31-33

Misconception #47

The Israelites were Always Slaves in Egypt Until Moses Led Them Out of Bondage

FADE IN: Act One. Once upon a time, there was a magical place called Tinsel Town, where they told marvelous tales of wonder etched on tablets of silver with the finger of God. And not only did it seem as though the images on the screen had come down from On-High, even the stories seemed to have descended from Heaven. That's because when pioneers of the cinema sought to elevate their fledgling industry beyond the status of mere nickelodeons, they hedged their bet by reworking the stories they found in their most beloved book, the book of all books: *The Bible*.

The stories they were particularly drawn to contained elements that lent themselves to the very thing that made the movies so unique in the first place—stories expressed through the magic of special effects. And when these marvelous spectacles were produced, some of the best received were miracle-laden stories drawn directly from Scripture, like *The Ten Commandments*, *King of Kings*, and *Ben-Hur*.

So it was that one of the most famous of all misconceptions ever to be blamed on *The Bible* was born, courtesy of none other than Hollywood. In this case, the film in question concerns the twice-made epic, produced in 1923 and 1956, by Cecil B. DeMille: *The Ten Commandments*. Here's how it goes.

As our story opens, the Israelites are struggling as slaves in abject poverty, completely dominated by their Egyptian overlords. From the moment they wake up to the moment they go to sleep, the Israelites are systematically brutalized. Too despairing to lift their heads even in prayer, God nevertheless hears their cries and decides to act; He deigns to raise up a savior to deliver them from bondage.

Before long, rumors of the coming of this Hebrew messiah find the ear of the Pharaoh, and hoping to avert the fulfillment of this prophecy, he orders every male Israelite infant to be drowned in the Nile River. But, in a dramatic twist that not even Hollywood could have concocted, the baby Moses floats into Pharaoh's court by way of the very river that was supposed to drown him.

Terrific stuff! You're still with me, right?

Good; then comes Act Two. Growing up in the court of Pharaoh, Moses never realizes that he's actually the son of Hebrew slaves, though for some strange reason he's smitten at the sight of their suffering.

Then, through an ironic turn of events, Moses discovers his true identity; and even though it means forfeiting the riches and power of Egyptian royalty, he chooses to follow God's call. After being slaves in Egypt for centuries, the Israelites' dream of being free suddenly seems possible, if only Moses can persuade Pharaoh to let them go.

So far, so good? Wonderful!

Act Three follows. Working hand in hand with God to rain down ten plagues upon Egypt, Moses induces Pharaoh to release the Israelites. A great mass of people vacate Egypt and begin their fateful trek to freedom, only to find that Pharaoh's army is chasing them. And because the Red Sea blocks their way of escape, the people turn to Moses once again. But fear not. Moses raises his staff, the breath of God parts the Red Sea, and the Israelites escape the onslaught of Pharaoh's army, which is then destroyed in a great avalanche of water—all courtesy of the best special effects that Hollywood can produce!

Wow, what a story! Who writes stuff like this? No wonder most people assume it wasn't made up by any mere mortal. It comes straight from The Good Book, as is, right? Well, sorry to burst your bubble, folks, but think again. The story, I'm afraid, has undergone some editing for the sake of heightening the drama. Here's what I mean.

Remember: According to the three laws of disinformation, the first order of business is to latch onto any truth that's firmly founded on actual Scripture. In this case, one couldn't hope to find a better example. Virtually the whole story as appropriated by Hollywood is in *The Bible*, but with one all-important variation. Tinsel Town's version has the Israelites portrayed as slaves from the beginning of the story, as if they'd never known any other condition in their history. The Scriptures, however, reveal that far from starting out as slaves during their Egyptian sojourn, they were once a great and powerful nation living and ruling in the midst of Egypt's heartland.

Now at first, this point of divergence may not seem important, but it actually makes all the difference in the world. I'll explain why a little later, but before I do, let's look at how Hollywood's version differs from that of Scripture.

Just like every great misconception of *The Bible*, a great motion picture requires certain key elements; it needs a powerful story arc to be great. That means, in the case of *The Ten Commandments*, the Israelites must begin in bondage en route to being released into freedom. Otherwise, without this clearly sequential storyline, the movie itself might fail to deliver on its own terms.

But the truth is: What works for Hollywood doesn't necessarily work for Scripture. Cecil B. DeMille may have insisted that the Israelites start out as slaves, but God obviously had a different story arc in mind. And He did so because He had an entirely different purpose to reveal to mankind than Mr. DeMille did.

Completely ignoring Hollywood's demands, the God of *The Bible* made sure that when the Israelites entered Egypt some four hundred and thirty years before the Exodus they were led by the cunning patriarch Jacob and his twelve sons.

Eventually, Jacob's most gifted son, Joseph, ascended to a position of immense power as Egypt's viceroy.

> And Pharaoh said to his servants: "Can we find anyone to compare with Joseph, a man in whom the Spirit of God dwells so powerfully?"
>
> Then Pharaoh said to Joseph: "Because God has shown you so much, there's no one as clever and wise as you. Therefore, you'll rule over all my people. Only my throne will be greater than yours. Today I've established you over the whole of Egypt."
>
> And Pharaoh took off the ring from his hand, and put it on Joseph's finger. Arraying him in royal clothing made of fine linen, he placed a gold chain around his neck. And Pharaoh had Joseph seated in the second chariot, which rode next to him, and the people cried out to him: "Bow your knee, everyone, because Pharaoh has made Joseph to be ruler over all Egypt."[26]

It was through Joseph's authority, then, that the Israelites became beneficiaries of the most fertile sections of the country, wielding untold influence over the land and its people. So began a new phase in Egyptian history, where one man and his family grew into a coalition of shepherd-kings, which eventually achieved the kind of greatness generally attributed only to gods and goddesses.

> During Joseph's reign in Egypt, the number of those from the line of Jacob who entered the land was just seventy people. But over time, the Israelites increased to such an extent that they multiplied and grew into a powerful nation, filling the entire land with their people.

---

[26] *Genesis* 41:38-43

Eventually, though, Joseph died, along with his brothers and his entire generation, and one day, a new Pharaoh rose up in Egypt who scorned the memory of Joseph and his deeds. He said, "Just look at all these Israelites. They're greater and more plentiful than we are. Come, let's deal wisely with them, or else they'll keep multiplying, and someday, if a war ever breaks out, they'll join with our enemies and turn against us. So let's get rid of them, once and for all."[27]

Within little more than a generation, their vengeful plan had succeeded beyond their wildest dreams, reducing the once-powerful coalition of shepherd-kings into a scattered, disintegrated rabble.

Flash forward many generations, and it's now as though the Israelites had always been slaves in Egypt. And so they remained in that dismal state until God raised up one of the most famous of all messianic figures, Moses, who galvanized this beleaguered bunch into a group that was finally ready to recapture the dignity that had been stolen from them so long ago.

There you have it, then. What a subtle yet critical distinction. The question, however: Is it really a distinction that matters?

Well, it matters if one cares about what *The Bible* is trying to accomplish. It matters when you consider the Scriptures are designed to reveal God's intention toward mankind, which in turn reveals what our attitude toward God should be. As such, an understanding of all that pertains to the slavery of these Israelites and their emancipation from Egypt is something of paramount importance.

It's important because whenever someone watches a movie about God's control over history, which is what *The Ten Commandments* is about, questions inevitably come to mind: What forces conspired to reduce the Israelites to this miserable condition? If God was as concerned about them as the movie purports, why did He just stand by as they sank into slavery? And finally, if He was capable of the miracles depicted in the last half of the film, why did He wait so long to perform them?

Only when we look to the context of *The Bible* do we find the answer to such questions. Far from portraying God as having abandoned His people through a lack of concern for them, the Scriptures reveal He was actually working out a much larger plan. As such, the plan of human redemption was never something that could be embraced within the length of a single lifetime. Rather, it's a plan that's been unfolding throughout the entire span of biblical history.

---

[27] *Exodus* 1:5-10

That's because the Israelites in Egypt weren't the only ones that God was concerned about; He was working toward rescuing humanity on a global scale. In other words, God's plan doesn't touch upon just one point in time, as it was perceived by Israel of old, but throughout all time, as it's perceived by every son and daughter of faith.

The writer of *The Book of Hebrews* had this very thing in mind when writing his letter. To him, the drama of Moses leading the Israelites from bondage to freedom was more than just a historical event. It was also a shadow of things to come, a glimpse into the future life and mission of One even greater than Moses, as alluded to in the following passage.

> That's why, my brothers, you who are partakers of the heavenly calling should always consider the Apostle and High Priest of our profession, Christ Jesus, Who was faithful to the One Who appointed Him, just as Moses was faithful in his house…
>
> Because every house is built by someone, but He Who built all things is God. And Moses was truly faithful in his house as a servant in order that a testimony of the things that he did would be spoken of afterward. But Christ is a Son over His own house, Whose house we are if we hold onto the confidence and joy of hope to the very end.[28]

What's more, the *Hebrews* author said:

> By faith, Moses, when he came of age, refused to be called the son of Pharaoh's daughter, choosing to suffer affliction with God's people rather than to enjoy the pleasures of sin for a season, having esteemed the reproach of Christ greater than all the treasures of Egypt, because he cared more about the reward he'd receive in the end.[29]

With the help of these passages, we can now begin to understand what Hollywood's version of these events could never hope to convey. In short, when the *Hebrews* writer described the actions of Moses, he clearly recognized that Moses wasn't acting in a vacuum. Instead, he saw him acting as a messianic figure in a long line of messianic figures—expressed in his statements that Moses "esteemed the reproach of Christ greater than the treasures of Egypt," and that he was "faithful in his house in order that a testimony of the things he did would be spoken of afterward."

---

[28] *Hebrews* 3:1-6
[29] Ibid. 11:24-26

In saying these things, the writer intended to convey something that even Moses could never have known at the time: In fulfilling his mission as *a* deliverer of Israel, he was, in reality, acting in direct relation to what Jesus would later fulfill in His role as *the* Deliverer of humanity.

The Apostle Matthew would also perceive a similar connection between past and present, in the events of the early years of Jesus as they pertained to the Exodus of Israel.

> And when the Three Wise Men had departed from the presence of King Herod, an angel of the Lord appeared to Joseph in a dream, saying, "Quickly, take your child and his mother, and flee into Egypt. There you're to remain until I bring you word, because Herod is going to try and kill the Child."
>
> So that night, he took his family, by cover of darkness, and departed into Egypt. And there they stayed until the death of Herod so that it might be fulfilled, which was spoken of the Lord by the prophet, saying, "Out of Egypt have I called My Son."[30]

In this verse, Matthew was referring to *The Book of Hosea*, where the prophet had God saying, "When Israel was yet a child, I loved him, and called My son out of Egypt."[31]

Thus, we see, for God, there's always a connection between the past and the present. And in this, we might finally see why it's so critical to understand that before the Children of Israel were ever slaves in Egypt, they first ruled and reigned as only royalty could. Then, and only then, will we be able to view history as God views it.

In short, in the events of the Exodus, Israel functioned as a "type" on multiple levels. In theological terms, typology is the doctrine that expounds the idea that certain events, persons, or statements in *The Old Testament* are "types" that represent "shadows" that pre-figure specific attributes relating to the Advent of Christ. Concerning the Exodus, Israel can be seen as a type of humanity in Adam, stripped of its royal status; as a type of the faithful, redeemed by divine deliverance; and as a type of Christ, led forth from Egypt as the beloved Son of the Father. As for Moses, he, too, functioned as a type of Christ, in his role as the Deliverer of Israel who willingly shed his royal status in order to perform his duties in concert with God's intervening actions.

In this cosmic drama of the ages, then, both Israel and Moses

---

[30] *Matthew* 2:13-15

[31] *Hosea* 1:1

represented shadows of things to come: Israel, as the Child of Faith, and Moses, as Christ Himself, Who relinquished His royal splendor, and taking on the form of a lowly servant—"a slave of Egypt," as it were—endured death before God raised Him to newness of life.

In all this, we see how God orchestrated a breathtaking drama of the ages, in which Moses miraculously brought Israel forth from out of the land equated in *The Bible* with the bondage of sin. We see Christ, the Redeemer, has rescued His band of the Faithful—in that generation, and in all generations. We tip our hats to the Master Director, the Lord of Hosts; we applaud.

Fade out: The End.

Misconception #46

God Sent Serpents After the Children of Israel as They Wandered Through the Wilderness

ACCORDING TO tradition, the God of Israel went to great lengths to induce the king of Egypt to allow the Israelite slaves to leave his country. First, He raised up Moses to lead the people. But when Pharaoh paid no attention to his demands, God sent ten plagues upon the land, inciting the king of Egypt to finally let them go.

Then, having escaped the pursuing Egyptian army by passing through the parted Red Sea, the Israelites began an arduous journey through the Sinai Desert. Before long, though, the people grew weary and began complaining to Moses that God didn't really know what He was doing by dragging them into the Wilderness with no provision for food or water.

Eventually, God got fed up with the Israelites and their constant complaining, so He decided to punish them by sending venomous snakes into their midst. Savagely bitten, left and right, many of the helpless people were killed. Only after Moses held up a staff of brass, forged in the likeness of a serpent—so that whoever looked at this uplifted staff was cured of their bite—did the suffering finally subside.[32]

Pretty wild story, don't you think? Ten plagues descending on the land of Egypt? Israelites escaping through a hole in the Red Sea? Venomous snake bites miraculously cured just by looking at a brass serpent? Can this stuff really be believed?

Well, considering that *The Bible* is a book full of miracles, the answer is yes we can. But that's not really the issue that seems so unbelievable to me.

What's unbelievable is: How could a God so determined to rescue the people of Israel turn against them so abruptly? It seems inconceivable that the Lord would go to such lengths to extricate them from slavery, and then proceed to capriciously mow them down with a bunch of venomous snakes. So what gives? Is there something more to this scenario that we're not hearing about?

---

[32] *Numbers* 21:4-9

Well, considering the constant forces of disinformation that seek to undermine a correct understanding of *The Bible*, yes, I do think so. And as usual, to determine what that is, we'll have to revisit this strange chapter of biblical history.

As we discovered in the previous essay, some four hundred and thirty years before the Exodus out of Egypt, the Israelites had entered the land under the leadership of Jacob and his sons. From a meager band of seventy people, they eventually became a tremendous nation. But once the patriarchs died, the Egyptians were able to regain everything they'd lost to the Israelites. Within a generation or so, they'd succeeded beyond their wildest dreams, reducing a network of once-powerful shepherd-kings into a disintegrated rabble.

Then, after more than three centuries of slavery, God raised up Moses, who reinvigorated them into a band of people who were finally ready to recapture their former glory. In a most startling fashion, the God of Israel struck at the heart of Egyptian power by sending ten plagues, in an attempt to break the will of the belligerent Pharaoh. But again and again, the Egyptian king refused to grant them freedom. Only after the firstborn of every male creature was killed—both human and animal—in what's now celebrated as the Day of Passover, did Pharaoh relent and free his precious slaves.

At this point, the Israelites made the most famous leg of their journey as Moses led them through the parted Red Sea, where they then found themselves smack dab in the middle of the Sinai Desert. Fortunately for them, Pharaoh's entire army was drowned in the process, so at least they'd never have to worry about them anymore.

What did worry them, though, was: Now that we're traveling through a desert, with no apparent source of food or water, what will become of us?

Just three days removed from the Red Sea, the people began to complain to Moses that there was no water. Immediately God had Moses lead them to two sources of water, first at Marah, where God sweetened waters that were originally too bitter to drink, and then to Elim, where the people found twelve wells from which to drink.[33]

Soon after, they began complaining that because there was no food to be found God might as well have left them to die in Egypt where they at least didn't have to contend with empty bellies. In response to their grumblings, God sent vast numbers of quail into their midst to feed them. Not only that, He provided them with a peculiar substance known as *manna*, a kind of bread that tasted like honey-filled wafers, which grew out of the ground as a form of plant life, with which the

---

[33] *Exodus* 15:22-27

people satisfied their hunger.[34]

The ironic thing about this series of events is, in hindsight it's obvious to us that the Lord was testing the faith of this fickle bunch of exiles. One minute the Israelites are about to be killed by Pharaoh's pursuing army, the next minute the Red Sea collapses on them and they're happy with God—for a while, that is.

Then, no sooner are they past the next series of trials, having been provided for with sweetened water, twelve wells, quail, and manna, the people find themselves without water yet again. But instead of giving God the benefit of the doubt, by having faith in Him and His ordained leader, what do they do?

> The people began to chide with Moses, saying, "How about giving us more water to drink?"
>
> And Moses replied, "Why are you giving me such a hard time? You're only irritating God with your belligerence!"
>
> But the people were so thirsty that they continued to press the matter, saying, "Is this why you brought us out of Egypt? So you could kill us and our cattle with thirst?"
>
> So Moses begged God: "What should I do with these people? They all want to stone me!"
>
> And the Lord told Moses: "Take the rod with which you parted the Red Sea and strike the rock in the sight of everyone."
>
> And water came forth from the rock in order to quench the thirst of the Israelites. That's why Moses named that place Meribah, (which means *provocation* or *strife*) because that's where the Israelites questioned whether or not the Lord was still with them.[35]

No wonder God got fed up, as *The Book of Hebrews* records:

> Today if you hear God's voice, don't harden your hearts, as it was in the day of provocation, in the Wilderness when your forefathers tempted Me, proved Me, and saw My works for forty years. And because of what they did to Me there, I was grieved with that generation, saying, "Their hearts are always in error regarding My ways, so I swore in My anger they wouldn't enter into My rest."[36]

And again:

---

[34] *Exodus* 16:3-36

[35] Ibid. 17:1-7

[36] *Hebrews* 3:7-11

With whom was God grieved for forty years? Wasn't it with those who sinned, whose carcasses fell in the Wilderness? And to those whom He swore they wouldn't enter into His rest, that is to say, those who wouldn't believe? So we see they couldn't enter in because of a lack of faith."[37]

So: How could a God so determined to rescue His people turn against them so abruptly? In retrospect, we can see He didn't act so abruptly, after all, did He?

With this new understanding in mind, let's continue our review.

The Israelites journeyed from Mount Hor, by way of the Red Sea, which encompassed the land of Edom, and there the people became discouraged again because the journey was so difficult. So the people started complaining about God and Moses, saying, "Is this why you brought us out of Egypt, to die in the Wilderness? There's no bread or water! And we hate this stuff you call manna!"

So the Lord sent fiery serpents among the people, and they bit them; and many died because of these bites. Then the people came to Moses, saying, "We've sinned, because we've spoken against the Lord, and against you; so pray to the Lord for us so He might remove the serpents from our midst."

And Moses prayed for the people, and God said to Moses: "Make a fiery serpent, and set it on a pole, so that if anyone who was bitten will look at it, they'll live."

So Moses made a serpent of brass and placed it on a pole, and whenever someone was bitten by a serpent, he merely had to look at the brazen serpent, and they lived.[38]

What do we have so far? We have a series of events that depict a benevolent God Who went to great lengths to rescue a people who obviously have a hard time appreciating what He did for them. Even though He rescued them from centuries of slavery, ushered them through the parted Red Sea, destroyed Pharaoh's pursuing army, and provided water and food at every point in their journey, they still had the nerve to put God on trial, as if He were their personal bellhop.

So what happened next? The Lord sent in the venomous snakes to get even with them, right?

Well, not exactly.

"What's that you say?" you might ask. "You mean God didn't

---

[37] *Hebrews* 3:17-19

[38] *Numbers* 21:4-9

send serpents after them? But isn't that what *The Bible* says?"

To which I'd reply, "It does if you accept the *King James* translation as it stands. It does if you ignore the context in which these events are described."

Let me take a moment to explain what I mean.

Once again, we have a passage in Scripture that falls short of its original intention due to a poor translation. In this case, the word used for "sent"—from the Hebrew word *shalach*—can just as easily be translated as "let loose" or "released."

So picture this: Instead of portraying a vindictive God spewing out serpents every which way, the more accurate version of this story is one in which the Israelites were wandering through the desert where thousands of serpents were already lurking about. After all, they were traveling through a desert, right? It'd be ludicrous to think there wouldn't be swarms of snakes lurking about, not to mention countless other venomous creatures just waiting to strike at a moment's notice. Yet not once is there any record of these creatures attacking the Israelites prior to this time. We can only assume, if no one was harmed, it was because God had preserved them the same way He had throughout their journey from Egypt.

With this new view in mind, we start to see a different spin to this whole wilderness experience. Now we see that, when the Israelites managed to weary God with their lack of faith, He simply "let loose" or "released" the thing He'd previously been holding back in His mercy.

The same thing happens when a loving father protects his children from harm's way until finally their persistent rebellion forces the father to allow them to discover the harsh realities of life he'd previously been protecting them from. In a case like that, no one would think that the father had blatantly struck out at his children. Why, then, would anyone think that God, the Father, would do what no earthly father would do?

So again, we ask: Why *would* we believe that a benevolent, loving God could be capable of such wanton acts of cruelty? The answer lies in the fact, as in previous cases, that centuries of tradition have caused most people to simply accept what the biblical translators—however well intentioned—have handed down to us. But consider some of the reasons why.

In previous ages of the world, humanity was thoroughly steeped in intolerance. As a result, it would've been much easier then than it is today to believe that the Deity could've acted so capriciously. Western culture was once captured by the Greco-Roman worldview, which was overrun with gods and goddesses who had no qualms about lashing out with human-like vengeance upon anyone who dared question their divine authority. Add to that the horrific legacy of the Spanish Inquisition, and one can easily understand how people might have viewed the supposed scope of God's wrath.

No wonder that the *King James* translators chose to offer this pessimistic interpretation of the tragic events as they seemed to be depicted in Scripture. Fortunately, though, when trying to determine the correct meaning of *The Bible*, we can overcome such errors by examining the original languages, as well as the context of the verses in question.

Finally, we need to look at one last thing if we're to catch a glimpse into why God allowed this disaster to occur in the first place. To the casual onlooker, this event seems like nothing more than a random act of violence in the Israelites' harrowing journey to the Promised Land. But to those who look past the surface, it's actually another of God's ways of foreshadowing future events, just as we saw in the previous chapter with the Israelites and Moses, who represented the faithful in Christ and Christ Himself, respectively. In this case, what we have is God entering into a moment of utter hopelessness in the lives of the Israelites and transforming it into a universal message of hope itself for all people and for all time.

How can we possibly know something like that?

We know because, one day, while Jesus was talking to His disciples about His impending death and resurrection, He provided a telling clue. Looking back to that wilderness experience, Jesus clearly saw God's purpose in all of it. He saw it because it wasn't just a story about Moses and a brass serpent on a pole; it was a story about Him and a destiny on a darkened hill. It was also a story not just of dying Israelites seeking an immediate cure but of a dying humanity seeking something far more important. Looking back and looking ahead, Jesus told His disciples ... and us:

> Even as Moses lifted up the brass serpent in the Wilderness, the Son of Man must also be lifted up so that whoever believes in Me won't perish but will have eternal life. Because God loved the world so much, He gave His only begotten Son so that whoever has faith in Me will never die but will have everlasting life.[39]

---

[39] *John* 3:14-16

Misconception #45

When Abraham Sought to Sacrifice Him, Isaac was Still a Child With No Idea What His Father was Planning

ONE OF THE MOST pervasive ideas mankind has about *The Bible* is that because it was written by so many different writers there's no point in believing in its so-called "divine" authorship. It's therefore assumed to be a fraudulent book, which only an idiot or a fool would treat as an object of trust.

On the face of it, this assumption seems reasonable; yet this thread of logic unravels in an instant when one considers the following alternative. Yes, *The Bible* was written by different authors, each writing from their own perspective, but this, in and of itself, doesn't negate the possibility of its divine origins. In fact, it's this very diversity that provides us with the clue that it can't possibly be the crude by-product of human inspiration.

What makes *The Bible* so amazing, actually, is that even though it's a book written across the entire span of human history, it still bears the unmistakable stamp of a single point of view. In other words, although so many hands have "stirred the pot," so to speak, the scriptural record as a whole still bears a remarkable similarity through in and throughout. From age to age, what begins as a germ of thought in *The Old Testament* unfolds with astonishing continuity in *The New Testament*. From author to author, every book in *The Bible* echoes with the same voice, unfolds the same storyline. And it's this fact that rings out to those with ears to hear and eyes to see: This is no coincidence; it is, in fact, the greatest proof of its divine authorship.

With this idea in mind, let's examine our next misconception, in another story that's troubled scholars and laypersons alike for generations. It involves one of the most famous dramas in *The Bible*, if only because it's commemorated by no less than three of the great religions of mankind—Judaism, Christianity, and Islam.

According to tradition, Abraham was ninety-nine years old when God visited him with good news of the birth of a son to be conceived by his wife Sarah, who was almost ninety years old at the time. Yet, in spite of a brief bout of skepticism, Sarah did conceive the following year, and Isaac was born, much to the couple's shock and delight.

Before long, the child was growing up, happy and healthy, but soon, unbeknownst to his wife and son, Abraham was again visited by God. This time, however, the Lord came as the bearer of bad news. The same child the Lord had bestowed upon Abraham and his wife would now have to be offered up to God as a burnt offering.

Although horrified, Abraham still determined to carry out the difficult task that the Lord demanded of him. So, without ever letting on to his intentions, Abraham took his young son from his doting mother and led him to Mount Moriah. And there, he prepared to sacrifice his beloved Isaac, in a sacred, howbeit bloody, ritual.

Fortunately, for all involved—as the story goes—God intervened at the last possible moment, staying the hand of Abraham just as he was about to kill the child. The Lord then provided a substitute victim, a ram caught in a thicket, which Abraham was told to slay in place of his son.

So Isaac was spared a grisly death that day, Abraham passed his supreme test of faith, and God saw that his chosen man was even willing to sacrifice his beloved son if He asked him to.

Another thrilling story with a happy ending, right? Well, yeah, sure. But what, exactly, was the point of the whole exercise, really?

Since its first telling, this story has had humanity scratching its collective head, wondering: What was God thinking in thrusting an innocent child into such a bizarre predicament?

We can only imagine the sheer terror Isaac must have felt as he watched in helpless confusion while his loving father held up that knife, poised to cut his throat.

But wait; before we go too far with our questions and doubts, certainly we're all acquainted with what the typical evangelical response has been throughout the ages. Immediately, they come to the Lord's defense, offering up their pat explanations, and all with a perfectly straight face: "Of course," they insist, "God never intended for Abraham to actually kill his son. This event was just a foreshadowing of what the Lord was planning to do with His Son Jesus. In this case, Isaac was acting as a type of the Son of God, Who would willingly offer Himself up as the Lamb of God, slain as a sacrifice for the sins of the world."

To which our reply to such profound wisdom is: "Gee, I never thought of it that way. Okay, sure, I see the parallel now."

There's only problem: When it comes to seeing the sacrifice of Isaac as a genuine shadow of things to come, an honest look at *The Book of Genesis* will actually reveal how deficient it is in that department.

Now before anyone condemns me as an unbelieving heretic, let me take this opportunity to review the traditional biblical landscape to prove my point. But do bear in mind, won't you, that in doing so, it isn't my intention to undermine the reality of Scripture's ability to portray these all-important types and shadows. On the contrary, it's my intention to absolutely prove its ability. But to do that, without needing smoke and mirrors to make these parallels work, there are certain things we need to be aware of.

First, we need to know that for Isaac to be a genuine shadow of things to come he would have had to endure whatever Jesus endured or else the notion of types and shadows becomes meaningless.

Now, it goes without saying that Jesus, as the pre-existent Lamb of God slain before the foundations of the world were laid, cannot be compared in every way to an antecedent such as the mortal Isaac. However, in terms of the human drama they both performed, I do believe they can be compared, as this certainly was the central issue in God's view.

For example, everyone knows that Jesus was a willing participant in His sacrificial offering at Golgotha. Again and again, He explained that no one could take His life if He hadn't been willing to offer it of His own accord. So, if Isaac were a genuine type of Christ, he, too, would've been a willing participant when Abraham took him to Mount Moriah. But clearly, the *Genesis* record lacks this critical dimension of the story.

According to it, Isaac is described as a mere lad who's completely ignorant of the drama in which he's been ensnared. If that's the case, then Isaac fulfills the function of a type about as much as a trained monkey led about on a rope. The idea of Isaac as a type of Christ, seen in this light, simply doesn't add up. And frankly, no amount of propaganda, no matter how many centuries it's been repeated, will ever convince me otherwise.

But no worries; as we've seen in the past, this doesn't always mean the end of the story. Fortunately, there's that other source of biblical truth that does so much to set things right; and just as fortunate, this source is available in nearly every modern bookstore. It's an ancient body of biblical wisdom called *pseudepigraphal* literature, better known as apocryphal literature. Among the various titles—all of which like *The First Book of Enoch* were considered God-inspired at some point in history—is a text we've previously investigated: *The Book of Jasher*.

In it is a detailed account of the life of Abraham—so detailed, in fact, that many scholars believe it provided the source material for the later, and obviously condensed, version that Moses produced, with his more familiar *Pentateuch*. More importantly, with *Jasher* as our backdrop, we'll be able to reconcile certain irreconcilable details concerning Isaac—details that help us link events in the lives of both

Abraham's son and God's Son. Here, then, is how we'll peel away centuries of disinformation and get to the real truth of the matter.

To begin with, *Jasher*, like *The Pentateuch*, describes Abraham and Sarah as being ninety-nine and eighty-nine years old, respectively, when God tells them about the impending birth of Isaac. In that regard, both the canonical and apocryphal accounts are identical. But they diverge where the apocryphal literature goes into much more detail in describing the lives of the biblical patriarchs. The most obvious example of this concerns their extended life spans.

According to *Jasher*, when Abraham was eighty-seven years old, his great, great-grandfather, Reu, the son of the patriarch Peleg, died at the age of two hundred and thirty-nine.[40] And when Isaac was one hundred and ten years old, the patriarch Shem, the son of Noah, died at the ripe old age of six hundred years old.[41]

Now it's important to realize that, according to this time frame, Abraham and Sarah would've been considered middle-aged when God told them they'd be having a son—something which needs mentioning because most *Bible* teaching neglects to emphasize this critical aspect of the Isaac story. And while this bit of information might seem unrelated right now, it will impact our story later on, so please tuck it away in your memory bank as we return to our original storyline. This time, though, upon returning let's weave into this scene the traditional view provided by *Genesis*, to highlight the difference between the two accounts.

So, after receiving news of a son being born to them, Abraham and Sarah couldn't help but be astonished at such a possibility. After all, Sarah had been barren her whole life, so that with each passing year, the hope of providing a son to Abraham grew dimmer still. If, in fact, she could conceive, as God's promise assured them, then it'd be considered a miraculous birth indeed. That's why Sarah laughed when she first heard the news of this impending birth. It's also why God insisted their special child be named Isaac, meaning "laughter," to commemorate her initial lack of faith in the face of God's promise.

And so it was that Isaac was born the following year, "even while his parents were yet stricken with old age"—at least that's the way that *Genesis* describes their condition. And it does so, mind you, in spite of the fact that the canonical record later records that Abraham lived until he was one hundred and seventy-five years old.[42]

Meanwhile, you're no doubt thinking: "Okay, all that's very

---

[40] *Jasher* 16:22

[41] Ibid. 28:24

[42] *Genesis* 25:7

interesting, but what's any of this got to do with whether or not Isaac is a true type of Christ?"

The first point is that, in establishing this often-overlooked aspect of extended life spans, something very important becomes obvious. It reveals how the miraculous quality of Sarah giving birth has been obscured by canonical tradition. With only *Genesis* as our reference point, we've always been led to believe that Isaac's birth was a miracle because Sarah was so old. But not so. It wasn't so much a miracle because she conceived Isaac at that so-called "advanced age" as it was because she'd been barren until that age. It doesn't change the fact that Isaac's birth was a miracle; it just changes the emphasis from Sarah's age to her barrenness.

The reason this distinction is so important is, according to *Genesis*, Isaac was an unwitting lad when Abraham led him to Mount Moriah. But if Isaac had been just a lad, we'd be facing another major stumbling block. Why? Because as a boy, Isaac wouldn't be a fitting parallel to the Man Jesus. As a child, Isaac would still have been under the jurisdiction of his father, and any decision he made would've been subject to Abraham's consent. This would clearly undermine any supposed parallel, then, between Isaac and Jesus.

But fear not. This is precisely why we're looking at *The Book of Jasher*, because it provides us with the necessary information we need to overcome this obstacle created by *Genesis*. What's more, the apocryphal record not only solves the problem of Isaac's age, but it also provides us with that other piece of the puzzle that's missing from the canonical record—the part where Moses characterized Isaac as being ignorant of why his father was taking him to Mount Moriah.

As for tradition that would have us believe Isaac was just a lad, *Jasher* reveals he was really thirty-seven years old when Abraham took him to Mount Moriah. Now immediately, some might argue that if Moses was wrong in telling us Isaac was a lad even though he was thirty-seven years old, this could undermine the belief that *The Bible* is the revealed word of God. But I say, not so, because in light of both the canonical and apocryphal accounts of the extended life spans of the patriarchs, Moses was quite accurate in describing Isaac as a lad—that is, when you remember to factor in a proper understanding of the lengthy life spans in those days.[43]

As for tradition that would have us believe Isaac was ignorant of his possible fate at the hands of his father, we can also thank *Jasher* for restoring a correct understanding. That's because just as depicting Isaac as a mere lad obscures the parallel between him and Jesus, the

---

[43] *Jasher* 22:41, 53

same problem arises if Isaac had been ignorant of his father's plan. But fortunately, *Jasher* paints a far different picture:

> One day, Isaac was talking with his brother Ishmael, who was bragging to him about how he'd been circumcised like their father Abraham when he was just thirteen years old.
>
> To which Isaac replied, "But, dear brother, you only sacrificed a small piece of your flesh for God. What's so special about that? I, on the other hand, would be willing to give my very life if God were to ask Father to offer me up as a burnt offering."
>
> And the Lord heard Isaac that day, and at that moment He decided to test Abraham in exactly that way.[44]

So you see, far from being an ignorant lad who was swept into a confusing ordeal by an overzealous father, the apocryphal literature reveals something that's been shrouded for centuries. The astonishing truth is: Isaac was the one who inadvertently set off the chain reaction of events.

Now, thanks to *Jasher*, we can see why Isaac can, and should, be regarded as a genuine type of Christ. Like Jesus, the Man, Who willingly offered Himself up on Golgotha, Isaac really was all that his divine counterpart was in life. Not a child but a man, not ignorant of his fate but fully aware of what he'd committed himself to.

What a shame, then, that tradition has lagged so far behind in conveying the full-orbed reality that *The Bible* has been revealing to us all along. Maybe now we can better appreciate the Scripture's ability to tie together every loose cord of prophecy. Instead of seeing the biblical record as a jumble of discordant authors, we might instead see a sublime harmony in the events it describes. Although it portrays countless lives that stream across the entire span of history, still each life unfolds to uniquely inform every other life. And considering the persistent pressure to doubt the authenticity of *The Bible*, it's always refreshing to know that when seen as a whole, it really does have the ability to corroborate itself on every level, from age to age, and from cover to cover.

---

[44] *Jasher* 22:42-45

Misconception #44

*Moses Spent Forty Years as a Lonely Shepherd
Before He Led Israel in the Exodus*

LIVING IN OUR modern age of mass communication, there are times when even the *King James* Version of *The Bible* can't be blamed for a great misconception. Sometimes the culprit lies with the mass media itself. More specifically, what I'm talking about is our motion picture tradition. Just as we saw how the movie *The Ten Commandments* solidified the erroneous idea that the Israelites were always slaves in Egypt until the Exodus, we're now faced with another bit of skewed history this film presents as historical fact.

Once more, Cecil B. DeMille is calling the shots instead of the Lord of Hosts.

According to Mr. DeMille, Moses was very happy growing up in the royal splendor of Pharaoh's court, until the day he discovered that he'd actually been born the son of Hebrew slaves. Suddenly finding himself torn between two ways of life, Moses chose to side with his beleaguered people, whom he saw ceaselessly toiling under the crack of Egyptian whips.

Then, upon seeing an Egyptian overlord whipping one of his Hebrew brethren, Moses boldly stepped forward and strangled the Egyptian with his own whip. For the crime of murdering an overlord of Egypt, Moses—who could've one day been Pharaoh himself—was sent to die in the Wilderness.

Weary and dismayed, Moses wandered for days through the blistering heat of the desert. Then, at the brink of death, he stumbled upon a well and was refreshed by its waters; there he met the seven daughters of Jethro, who happily provided him safe haven.

For the next forty years—so the story goes—Moses worked tirelessly as a shepherd in the land of Midian, where he lived as a stranger among the people, until the Lord appeared to him in a burning bush. It was then that God explained to Moses that he'd been chosen to lead the Children of Israel out of Egyptian bondage.[45] Stunned at such a proposition, Moses hemmed and hawed: "Why, Lord?" "Why

---

[45] *Acts* 7:30-35

would You send me?" "Who am I to lead Your people?" "What will I tell them when they ask Who sent me?" On and on he went, trying his best to let God know He was choosing the wrong man for the job, because, as a potential deliverer, he simply had no credentials. But apparently God wasn't going to be dissuaded, so, like every great story, the hero finally put aside his doubts and fears, and embraced the mission; off he went, back to the land of his birth.

Returning to the court of Pharaoh, Moses then squared off with the most powerful nation of the day, and in the end pulled off the miracle of the century—with God's help, naturally.

And everybody lived happily ever after; roll credits.

As usual, there's nothing quite like a good Hollywood yarn to make one feel warm and fuzzy, is there? You get to watch a great movie, and while you're at it, you go away feeling like you've learned something about *The Bible* in the process. It's a win-win situation all the way around. Who can complain about that, right?

Only problem is: As you can imagine, there's so much more to this tale than meets the eye. After all, that's the point of all these essays on misconceptions, right? So what's wrong with this picture?

The problem lies, once again, in our endless desire to excise our favorite versions of the stories in *The Bible*, and to treat them as if they're the only ones that exist. The only pitfall in doing that is, the Scriptures were written like every other book of history. By that I mean, there isn't just one book written about Abraham Lincoln; there are many books about his life and death. Some focus on his fabled upbringing in a log cabin, where he learned to read by candlelight; others for on the tragic side of his presidency, which ended in his assassination at the hands of an infamous zealot.

The Bible is no different in this regard. It's well known, for example, that in *The Old Testament*, the books of *Kings* and *Chronicles* cover the history of God's people in the Promised Land, but they do so from different perspectives. *The Book of Kings* focuses on the northern kingdom of Israel; *The Book of Chronicles*, on the southern kingdom of Judah. Both books examine the same period of history, yet each focuses on specific story elements from their own point of view.

Likewise, the story of Moses' journey of faith, leading him from the court of Pharaoh to the desert hideaway and back again, has also been retold in several different versions in the scriptural record. In the canonical record, we find *The Old Testament* accounts in *Exodus*, *Leviticus*, *Numbers*, and *Deuteronomy*, and in *The New Testament*, we find accounts in *Acts* and *Hebrews*. We also just discovered there's another even more revealing source of biblical history. Just as we read a more in-depth rendition of Abraham and Isaac's life in *The Book of Jasher*, we can find a more detailed version of Moses' life there, too.

There, we discover that during the forty-year period of apparent obscurity that Moses experienced in the Wilderness—where he allegedly lived as a simple shepherd—the *Jasher* account paints a much different picture of what was happening in the life of the once-and-future-deliverer of Israel.

According to *Jasher*, a war was raging between the people of Aram and Cush at the same time that Moses first left Egypt. From there, he went to the land of Cush, where the king and princes found that Moses was a great and worthy fighter among their troops. To them, he was like a lion in battle, and soon he became the king's counselor.

After several years with them, the king of Cush died unexpectedly, and the people made Moses their new king, even going so far as to give him the wife of their dead king as a bride.[46]

For forty years, Moses reigned over the land of Cush, as the Lord had granted Him divine favor in the sight of all the people. But even as Moses sat upon the throne, he never forgot the God of his forefathers, so much so that he avoided conjugal relations with his new queen, recalling how Abraham had forbidden his sons to take wives from the daughters of Canaan. Moses even restrained from falling in love with the queen, preferring to follow the Lord with all his heart and mind.

So it was that during his forty years as king—an account that admittedly differs from that of *Genesis* and *Acts*—Moses accomplished many great things because the Lord was with him.[47] He prospered in his kingdom, conducting the government of Cush in justice and integrity, and so the people both loved him for his deeds and feared him for his prowess.

Meanwhile, however, the queen grew jealous of Moses' power, resentful over his blatant disregard for her. In the fortieth year of Moses' reign, she instigated a rebellion against her husband, citing his disloyalty to the gods of Cush. "It's far better," she said, "for my son to reign over you than this slave of the king of Egypt."

But the people of Cush were afraid to revolt against their beloved king, so they couldn't bring themselves to disparage him or harm him in any way. Instead, they lavished him with great honor and splendid gifts, and sent him on his way.

So Moses left the land of Cush, because—says *Jasher*—it was according to the Lord's plan, as it was now the appointed time for which God had destined him to lead the Israelites from the affliction

---

[46] *Jasher* 72:21-37

[47] Ibid. 73:30-48

of Egypt.[48]

When we take the time to look, then, we see that God knew exactly what He was doing when He called Moses into action as the deliverer of Israel.

At this point, however, we're faced with a mystery. If Moses did write *The Pentateuch*—as I believe he did—what could've compelled him to leave out this chapter of his life? Was he doing what any other storyteller would've done faced with a similar situation? Meaning: Was he trying to emphasize God's role in rescuing the Children of Israel while trying to de-emphasize his own?

Well, if he was, he certainly didn't have to. *The Bible* is full of instances where God chose individuals whom He trained to do certain jobs before He called them to greater tasks later in their lives. Before his confrontation with Goliath, David killed a lion—not to mention his time as a mere shepherd en route to becoming ruler over all Israel. Then there were many of Jesus' disciples who apprenticed as fishermen before the Lord called them to become fishers of men.

Again and again, we find this happening. *The Book of Hebrews* in particular speaks of this, when it uses a word that in the Greek is a derivative of the English words to "train" or "nurture." It's used no less than six times in seven verses in the twelfth chapter of *Hebrews*. The Greek word used there is *paidea*, meaning "to chasten," which denotes the way a schoolmaster trains or nurtures a child.

In our modern view, the word "chasten" brings to mind everything negative and abrasive. But in the context of God's plan, it connotes His divinely-inspired ways of training us, trial by trial, all the while nurturing us toward a deeper awareness of His control over our lives. As the writer of *Hebrews* exhorted us:

> Don't despise the chastening of the Lord, or faint when He rebukes you, because the Lord chastens everyone He loves, scourging every child whom He receives. But if you endure this chastening God promises to deal with you as with His own children, because what children are they that have never been discipline by their father? Without being disciplined, who are you really? You're nobody's child; you're a bastard!
>
> What's more, we've all had earthly fathers who've corrected us, and still we honored them in what they did. In the same way, shouldn't we be happier to subject ourselves to the Father of spirits, and live?
>
> When our earthly fathers disciplined us in the short time

---

[48] *Jasher* 76:1-12

> they had with us, they did the best they could because they didn't know any better; but when God disciplines us, He knows exactly what He's doing, so that ultimately we might share in His holiness.
>
> So, yes, it's true: No chastening brings us any happiness while it's upon us. All we know is that we're suffering; but after the pain is over, those of us who've been exercised by its efforts bear the fruit of righteousness.[49]

These verses show us, then, that it's God's way to lead us from small tests of faith to larger ones, so that each trial we face prepares us for the next one. What we see in this is something akin to the way a manager trains a boxer. First, they have them fight against several lesser skilled opponents, and then gradually, over time, they have them fighting a series of more highly skilled ones.

That's clearly what God did with Moses.

Far from calling him to a task that was beyond his ability, the Lord had trained him in that forty-year wilderness experience to know exactly what it was like to lead a great mass of people through the challenges that faced them in that day and age. So when Moses bantered with God over his mission to lead the Israelites in the Exodus, he was nothing like the raw greenhorn that tradition has led us to believe. In fact, he was acting like any war-weary veteran in that situation. He knew he was qualified for his next mission; he just needed a push in the right direction. And as for God, He knew exactly why He'd chosen Moses, because he was someone He'd been training, hand in hand, for four decades in the wilderness of Cush.

So once again we see just how the bricks and mortar of disinformation build up a wall of confusion that distorts the truth of Scripture as God intends us to receive it. But fortunately, as thinking creatures, we can also rightly divide the word of truth to get a clearer picture of what *The Bible* really says.

In this case, we find an overlooked source of biblical wisdom has again come to our rescue. Thanks to apocryphal texts like *The Book of Jasher*—or I should say, thanks to their being overlooked—we can see how this misconception about a pivotal aspect of Moses' life has been created. More importantly, we see, when we're willing to re-examine such extra-biblical sources, how this disinformation undermines even the most important tenets of scriptural truth.

As a result, no less than two critical points, which constitute twin aspects of a major theme found throughout *The Bible*, are lost. Not only

---

[49] *Hebrews* 12:5-11

does this misconception suppress the exploits of Moses as a worthy deliverer-in-training in Cush for forty years, but it also ignores what *The Book of Hebrews* says about God's habit of training His called ones. When God chooses someone to do a job for Him, He first trains them as any loving father would, whether it's Moses called to a great mission like leading the Children of Israel to freedom, or a faithful believer called to discover their own unique place in the greater plan of God's deliverance for humanity.

Misconception #43

*Only Humans Get into Heaven;
Sorry, No Pets Allowed*

ASK ANY CHRISTIAN if they think their pets are going to Heaven, and nine out of ten of them will probably tell you the same thing: "Gee, I guess not, because *The Bible* says you've got to have faith to get in. I mean, sure, God created the animals, but that doesn't prove they'll get into Heaven. That's reserved for people who have a personal relationship with Him, right? How can animals know God the same way humans can?"

Admittedly, on the surface, all this sounds quite logical. Or at least it does as long as you're content with an oversimplified view of biblical reality. But beware: You might be falling far short of what the whole Book of God says about who gets into Heaven.

How about you? Are you really so sure this issue is that cut-and-dry? And could *The Bible* be that vague about such a vast portion of His creation? Let's take a moment, then, to search the Scriptures for any clues toward solving this mystery.

The first chapter of *Genesis* depicts a world in which God first created the animals and then mankind. And when He'd finished: "The Lord found that everything He'd created was good."[50]

What's more, the Scriptures reveal that God created the animals out of the very same material from which He created Adam. To confirm this, let's re-examine some familiar biblical territory.

> The Lord said, "It isn't good that the man should be alone, so I'll make companions for him." And out of the *ground* God formed every beast of the field, along with every fowl of the air. And He brought them before Adam to see what he'd call them; and whatever Adam decided to call them that was to be their name.[51]

So, what's this word used for the "ground" from which the animals were created? The word in the Hebrew just happens to be *adamah*,

---

[50] *Genesis* 1:20-31
[51] Ibid. 2:18-19

which, according to *Strong's Exhaustive Concordance*, comes from the root word *adam*, meaning "ground." How ironic is that? The biblical word for the material God used to create these companions for humanity is actually a derivative of the word for Adam himself.

Could this be why scientists were able to discover a link between the biology of the human and animal kingdoms so essential in their ongoing search for cures to disease? And could this connection between human and animal genetics explain why the "theory" of evolution is so irresistible to the scientific community?

Also noteworthy about this verse is the way it states, in no uncertain terms, that God specifically created animals as companions for humanity, not as slaves—as tradition so often insists—and certainly not as food.

So much for the notion, then, that it's *The Bible* that insists that God views humanity as being inherently superior to the animal kingdom. To the contrary, when God said everything He created was good in His sight, He meant *everything!*

What a shame that most people simply accept the idea that God only created animals to be tools for the sake of His greater creation of humanity. How arrogant are those who choose to hunt and peck at Scripture, ignoring anything that doesn't support their lopsided interpretation of what they'd like the Scriptures to say.

But such is the power of the three laws of disinformation: Latch, isolate, and repeat.

And to think: How many centuries have rolled by that continue to distort the fallen aspect of the Adamic portion of creation in a way that denigrates the rest of the non-Adamic, which God Himself saw as being good?

Now, this certainly doesn't mean that the animal kingdom hasn't suffered because of God cursing Adam and his descendants. Any biblical scholar would readily admit the Apostle Paul was speaking the truth when he said that both the animal and human kingdoms are linked in relation to the Fall of Adam. Speaking to this point, in *The Book of Romans*, Paul wrote:

> Every living creature waits expectantly for the manifestation of the children of God, seeing as how even the animals were made subject to pride, not willingly, but because of Him Who subjected them in hope, because *every creature* will *be delivered* from the bondage of corruption into the glorious liberty of God's family. Until then, we see how the entire creation groans and agonizes in pain together, and not only them, but we, too, which have the first fruits of the Spirit, even we who

yearn within ourselves, waiting for the adoption, that is, for the redemption of our bodies.[52]

So, from *The Old Testament* to *The New Testament*, the Scriptures are clear. God created the animal and human kingdoms out of the very same material, and He created them in a purposefully united way. To believe otherwise would be to buy into the kind of faulty thinking that only people who are themselves avid proponents of disinformation would gladly believe and embrace.

Not only that but, based on this way of thinking, we'd also have to dismiss what *The Bible* says about some rather unique encounters between animals and people. In this case, I'm not talking about tall tales of Scripture that are to be seen as *fish tales* but, instead, the kind that are meant to astonish and amaze, and, in doing so, persuade us to believe and embrace the miraculous.

Case in point: In *Genesis*, Eve encountered a talking serpent, but oddly enough, she never even acted startled. Without batting an eye, she just carried on a conversation with the creature as if nothing unusual at all was happening.

> Now the serpent was the cleverest animal that God had created, and he said to the woman, "Did God really say, 'You shouldn't eat from any of the trees in the garden'?"
>
> And the woman replied, "We can eat from any tree in the garden. God only told us to not eat from the tree at its center. That's the one He told us to avoid, because if we so much as touch it, we'll die."
>
> "Ah, you won't die," cooed the serpent. "It's just that God knows if you eat from that tree your eyes will opened, and you'll be just like God, knowing good and evil.[53]

Likewise, in *The Book of Numbers*, we read:

> And when Balaam struck his donkey, the creature looked back at Balaam and asked, "What did I do to deserve that?"
>
> And Balaam replied, "You mocked me! And if I had a sword in my hand, I'd kill you, here and now!"
>
> Dumbfounded, the donkey blurted, "Who me? But aren't I your donkey? The one you've ridden ever since you got me? Have I ever done anything like that to you before?"
>
> And Balaam said, "Never!"[54]

---

[52] *Romans* 8:19-23

[53] *Genesis* 3:1-5

[54] *Numbers* 22:28-30

How bizarre is that? And when I say bizarre, I'm sure most of you think I'm asking: How bizarre is that for someone to have a conversation with a donkey or a serpent? But no; that's not what I'm saying at all. What I'm asking is: How bizarre is that for someone to so casually respond to a talking animal? No doubt talking to an animal is bizarre, I grant you. But considering that *The Bible* is a book full of miracles, the idea of a talking animal is certainly no harder to believe in than the parting of the Red Sea, or Jesus walking on water, or any other number of miraculous events. No, what I find so bizarre is the casual way that Eve and Balaam respond to these talking animals, as if they were carrying on a conversation with another human being.

Still, I can imagine many people reading this who are saying, "Ridiculous. No wonder we don't look to *The Old Testament* anymore for truly inspired wisdom. You can't really expect us to take stock in old wives tales like that anymore, can you?"

To which I'd reply, "Well, okay. Ever heard of *The Book of Revelation*? You believe in it—it's in *The New Testament*, right?"

"Of course," you'd say. "I believe it. Why do you ask?"

Well, let's see. Turn please to the opening chapters of *Revelation*, where the Apostle John is taken up to Heaven, to the very throne of God. Notice how there are what are described as Four Beasts, sometimes called Four Living Creatures in the presence of the Lord Almighty; and these so-called "creatures" are said to resemble a lion, a bull, a man, and an eagle, respectively.[55]

> And I saw that near the throne of God, there were Four Beasts, and in the midst of the twenty-four Elders there stood a Lamb, as though it had been slain, having seven horns and seven eyes, which are the seven Spirits of God that have been sent forth throughout the entire world.[56]

Almost every *Bible*-believing Christian is familiar with these Four Living Creatures, but how many have ever stopped to consider how much talking they did in God's presence?

> And when I saw that the Lamb had opened one of the seals, I heard, like the sound of thunder, one of the Four Creatures saying, "Come and see." And look, a white horse...
> And when He'd opened the second seal, I heard the second Beast say, "Come and see." And there went out another horse that was red...

---

[55] *Revelation* 4:7

[56] Ibid. 5:6

> And when the Lamb had opened the third seal, I heard the third Creature say, "Come and see." And look, a black horse...
>
> And when He'd opened the fourth seal, I heard the voice of the fourth Beast say, "Come and see." And then I saw a pale horse."[57]

So not only does *The Bible* depict these Four Creatures as talking, but it also reveals that they're the driving force behind one of the most pivotal events in biblical history. And mind you, this event is so famous many unbelievers are familiar with it—the announcement of The Four Horsemen of the Apocalypse onto the world stage!

Still, some of you might be saying, "But wait. We're not talking about real animals here, are we? Doesn't *The Bible* say these are angels who only resemble the various animals described by John?"

To which I'd respond with a proviso and a follow-up.

First, my proviso, which comes in the form of a series of questions: If there really is such a huge difference between animals and angels, then why would there be any relationship between these two distinct species in Heaven? Is it because there really is a genuine connection between the two? And could this be why one of the angels among these Living Creatures is described as looking not like a lion, not like a bull, not like an eagle—but like a man?

As for my follow-up, I'd like to add that in *Revelation* there's another pivotal event involving animals. This scene, however, doesn't involve angels who simply resemble animals. It involves the genuine article—though John does describe them as doing some pretty *non-*animalistic things. Not only that but, like the Four Horsemen of the Apocalypse, this is one of the most famous events ever described in *The Bible*. Yet the fact that it involves real animals apparently does nothing to persuade the typical believer that—if they do consider themselves *Bible*-believers—they should believe the truth of this scene, too.

> I saw Heaven opened, and look, there was a white horse. He Who rode upon it was called Faithful and True, and in righteousness He judges and makes war... His Name is the Word of God, and the armies of Heaven that follow Him are all upon white horses, clothed with fine linen, white and pure.[58]

Now, admittedly, these white horses that Jesus and the returning

---

[57] *Revelation* 6:1-8

[58] Ibid. 19:11-14

saints are riding on are, unlike typical horses, flying through the air. Still they're described not as angels who happen to look like horses but actual flesh-and-blood horses. To this fact some of the greatest works of Christian art magnificently attest.

So the next time someone tells you animals form an inferior substrata in God's creation, you can explain to them that they, too, have fallen victim to a subtle form of disinformation. Next time, you'll know what to say to someone who tells you that because there are no animals in Heaven you can forget about seeing your beloved pets there when you arrive. And if anyone asks you why so many people believe these marvelous creatures that God made were devalued in the first place, you can tell them: Don't blame *The Bible*; blame the ones who've eagerly listened to the latch-isolate-and-repeat crowd for so many centuries.

What's more, anyone who wishes to see what *The Bible* says on this subject can turn to the twelfth chapter of *The Book of Exodus*. That's where they'll see how, at the first Passover Feast, God promised to spare the firstborn of not only every male child in Israel but all their male animals, too.

> The Lord said to Moses: "Consecrate to Me every firstborn male, because the first offspring of every womb among the Israelites belongs to Me, whether human or animal."
>
> Then Moses said to the people, "Commemorate this day that you came out of Egypt, out of the land of slavery, because the Lord brought you out with a mighty hand...
>
> "And when any of your sons ask you in the days to come: 'What is this?' You tell him: 'We were delivered from Egypt, from the house of bondage, by the strong hand of the Lord. As it so happened, when Pharaoh didn't want to let us go that the Lord killed all the firstborn in Egypt—of both man and beast. That's why we sacrifice to the Lord *every male creature* that opens the matrix of the womb, and why all our firstborn sons are redeemed.'"[59]

The real significance of all this lies in the fact that, as any biblical scholar will tell you, God intended this Passover event—involving the slaying of a lamb—to typify the death of Christ, Who was Himself the true Lamb of God. On that night, any family who trusted God by smearing the blood of the Pascal lamb on the doorposts of their homes was spared the death of their firstborn males, both humans and animals. Just imagine, then, if the blood of the Passover lamb

---

[59] *Exodus* 13:1-3, 14-15

accomplished so great a salvation, how much more effective is the shed blood of God's Son in providing a ransom for the families who place their trust in Christ Jesus?

So, again, when anyone tries to tell you that God's word says humans are more important than animals, tell them not to blame *The Bible*; blame it on those misguided ones who insist on reducing Scripture to their own puny image. Blame it on those ways of thinking that forever minimize God's true view of things.

Instead of viewing animals as being inferior to mankind, realize that the Scriptures can never be used to condone the slaughter of the animal kingdom, as if we were given free license over animals because of some inherent superiority we possess.

Realize, too, that this subjection of the animal kingdom is just a temporary detour. That's because it didn't happen because of any crime the animals committed—to echo the words of Paul—but "because of human pride." But, thank God, "by reason of Him Who subjected us in hope, *every creature* will *be delivered* from the bondage of corruption."

In pointing to this connection between the destiny of humans and animals, Paul was making a critical point: The plight of the animal kingdom is actually a mirror of truth that speaks of our own tragic existence—glaring proof of the fallen nature of humans as but one species amidst a marred creation.

Therefore, we should always remember to gaze deeply into this mirror and to look honestly at our true selves. As fellow travelers in a vast Universe that groans together for the release of God's curse, we should never forget that our fate is inescapably linked to that of our animal counterparts. And therefore we should always strive to treat them as an extension of ourselves, even as God has ordained to treat us an extension of Himself.

Till then, we should keep in mind we're to do this not for our sakes alone, but for the sake of Jesus, Who sacrificed His own life to reconcile to Himself all creatures, great and small. And above all, we're to remember that only through the blood of the Lamb are we granted entrance into that most sacred place where each heart hopes to be reunited with every loved one we've ever known and lost, be they of our human or animal family.

Misconception #42

*All Students of The Zodiac are
Fools or Heretics*

IF EVER THERE was a perfect case study in the power of disinformation, this is it. More than any other, the controversy over whether there's a message in the stars—a.k.a. The Zodiac—presents us with the ideal model of how a great misconception can blot out some of the richest aspects of God's revelation. The only reason it doesn't appear further up on this list is because it's also among the most overlooked areas of discussion. If the subject of The Zodiac is even hinted at in casual conversation, it's instantly dismissed as having anything to say to Scripture-loving Christians.

But as always, this tendency to avoid such a spectacular aspect of God's creative power has me itching to dive right in. For the life of me I can't help wondering: "What's all the fuss about? Does anybody who believes in God as the Creator of the Universe actually think the devil made the stars? And if this Creator God did adorn the Heavens with His starry objects, wouldn't He have intended them to reveal His divine purpose in some special way?"

With questions like these in mind, let's examine what popular opinion says about The Zodiac, and from there, we'll proceed to Scripture.

The question of whether or not God created the stars of Heaven for a special purpose hinges primarily on a particular culture's attitude about His role in the Universe.

An early fringe sect of Christianity called Gnosticism rejected the notion that the God of *The Old Testament* created the Heavens and the Earth, insisting that a lesser Deity created them. This was their way of accounting for evil in the world, which they saw as inherently corrupt and therefore incapable of revealing any genuine truth about God. Thus, the possibility of any revelatory aspects of The Zodiac were negated because it was inconsistent with the Universe as they saw it.

In contrast, other cultures, such as those of medieval Europe, accepted the idea that God created the Heavens and the Earth as His unique vessel. However, despite the fact that God created the Heavens, any message The Zodiac might have communicated to humanity was marred by the intervention of evil entities like Satan and his demonic minions, and so was lost forever in the mists of time.

Somewhere in between these two extremes, then, you'll find most people's opinion about The Zodiac.

Of course, even when a person is liable to accept the idea that the stars have the ability to communicate a message to humanity, it's never thought to be a biblically-oriented message—certainly not one that speaks of God's control over His purposeful Universe. Instead, it's a message intended to guide someone toward some merely human-oriented goal, such as which job to take, who to marry, or something to that effect.

Naturally, anyone mounting their campaign of disinformation would instantly dismiss the idea of a divine message in the stars by reminding us of every abuse of this kind, which is clearly condemned throughout Scripture. No doubt they'd point to what happened to the Jews during their Babylonian captivity, to those who'd been desperately seeking a way out of their miserable condition. When they'd grown tired of receiving words of truth the Lord was offering them, they couldn't resist the temptation to seek guidance from other sources. But no sooner had they done so than they received a grim warning from the prophet Isaiah:

> You've become weary because of all the false advice you've been seeking. Have it your own way then. Let the astrologers, the stargazers, and the fortune tellers try and save you from all the things that are about to come upon you. Look at how you'll all be reduced to stubble. The fire will burn you, and you'll be quite unable to deliver yourselves from the power of the flame.[60]

By hammering away at every abuse, such as those just described, one can't help but achieve the desired result. Above all, never allow anyone to even consider the possibility that God could've intended there to be a relationship between the written message in *The Bible* and the pictorial message in The Zodiac.

So goes the verdict: Think you see a message in the stars? Then you, too, should be ridiculed as a fool or condemned as a heretic. Or, at best, you should be written off as a nut.

But wait; are you absolutely sure that's what the God of *The Bible* wants? Just because so many have distorted the meaning of The Zodiac to serve their own selfish purposes, could there actually be more to this picture than meets the eye?

Fortunately, the Scriptures themselves are always capable of

---

[60] *Isaiah* 47:13-14

providing the truth concerning such important matters. Let's look at them to see if they can provide us with an antidote against the poison of latch-isolate-and-repeat.

To begin with, the prophet Amos told us: "Seek Him Who made the Seven Stars (referring to the Pleiades) and Orion."[61] The psalmist said: "God knows exactly how many stars there are, having given each and every one a name of its own."[62] And when Job pondered the majesty of God, he declared:

> It's God Who sealed up the stars and He alone Who spread out the Heavens, Who made Arcturus, Orion, and the Pleiades. God does great things beyond our understanding; yes, and wonders without number.[63]

The word "wonders," from the Hebrew word *pala*, describes things that are, by implication, marvelous, difficult, or hidden.

So, if it really was God Who created the stars, and not the devil, then why did He place these wonders—with all their marvelously difficult and hidden meaning—in the night sky?

> And God said, "Let there be lights in the firmament of the Heaven to divide the day from the night; and let them be for signs and for seasons, and for days and for years."[64]

Right from the start, then, God didn't create the stars just to mark the transition from day to night, to determine one season from another, or to denote which year we were living in. He also created them to act as "signs." In fact, the first time the Scriptures refer to a "sign," it's used in relation to the stars God placed in the Heavens.

According to *Strong's Exhaustive Concordance*, the Hebrew word for "sign" is *owth*, which means a "signal" (literally or figuratively), as a "flag," "beacon," "monument," "omen," or "evidence." By using this word *owth*, to describe God's purpose in creating the stars, *The Bible* clearly conveys the idea these signs were designed to reveal something very specific. So, what is God's specific message displayed in these signs?

King David, in writing *Psalm 19*, said:

> The Heavens declare the glory of God, and the firmament reveals His handiwork. From day to day, it speaks forth; night

---

[61] *Amos* 5:8

[62] *Psalm* 147:4

[63] *Job* 9:7-10

[64] *Genesis* 1:14

after night, it displays knowledge. There's no place on Earth, in which speech and language exist, that its voice isn't heard. Its message resounds throughout the whole world, and its conversation reaches to every corner of the globe.[65]

Interestingly enough, the Hebrew word here for "knowledge," which the Heavens are said to display each night, is a word that's derived from the root word *yada*, a unique word that conveys a variety of meanings. It speaks of the ability to learn something through observation, including the discovery of something to be understood figuratively, literally, euphemistically, and inferentially (particularly via recognition through careful consideration). And it's a knowledge that comes as the result of a declaration of instruction and that requires discernment in receiving that instruction.

Based on this, then, we'd have to admit that God Himself expected us to pay attention to what He was trying to convey via His starry messengers. So what could that message be? Is it a message intended for everyone? Or is it some special revelation that only an elite few will be able to understand?

Let's resume the task of piecing this puzzle together.

Remember: "The Heavens declare the glory of God." What's the glory of God?

The Apostle John said, "The Word became flesh and dwelled among us. We've seen His glory—the glory of the one and only Son from the Father, full of grace and truth."[66] And the writer of *The Book of Hebrews* declared, "The Son is the radiance of God's glory and the exact representation of His being."[67]

So, if Jesus is the glory of God, then it follows that the Heavens should declare Jesus, the Son of God.

Sure enough, as we piece together the puzzle, we do find that the message conveyed in The Zodiac reveals the story of Christ, the Redeemer. In fact, when we look at the evidence—both scripturally and astronomically—we find a perfect correspondence with the symbolism in each dimension of God's creation.

The most graphic example of this symbolic correspondence is revealed when we look at the Four Living Creatures described in *The Book of Revelation* and compare them with their scriptural counterparts in *The Old Testament*. To do this, let's begin in the second chapter of *The Book of Numbers*:

---

[65] *Psalm* 19:1-4

[66] *John* 1:14

[67] *Hebrews* 1:3

The Lord spoke to Moses and Aaron, explaining that, with the Tabernacle at its center, all the tribes of Israel are to set up their camps around it, with every tribe marking their camp with the standard according to his father's name.[68]

In the case of Judah, to the east, their standard was that of a lion; to the south was Reuben, whose standard was a man; to the west was Ephraim, whose standard was a bull; and to the north was Dan, whose standard was an eagle, or, its natural enemy, a snake or a scorpion.

Next we turn to the way these standards of the four tribes of Israel aren't grounded just in scriptural terms but also in astronomical terms. And we find this in a place where most Christians would never think to look—a Jewish synagogue. More specifically, we find it in the mosaic floor inside the Bet Alpha Synagogue, constructed in northern Israel around the sixth century. There, a zodiacal wheel portrays each of the four cardinal points, in correspondence with each of the four chief tribes of Israel: There's the lion of Judah, next to Leo; the man of Reuben, next to Aquarius; the bull of Ephraim, next to Taurus; and the scorpion of Dan, next to Scorpio. A picture of this zodiacal wheel can be seen on page fifteen of the book *The High Holy Days*. This floor plan even depicts the four cardinal signs of The Zodiac in relation to the months we're so familiar with: Leo with July-August, Aquarius with January-February, Taurus with April-May, and Scorpio with October-November.

The real significance of this association of imagery, between the chief tribes of Israel and their zodiacal counterparts, lies in the way it corresponds with the imagery in *Revelation*, where John describes four Living Creatures around the throne of God. In fact, four angels, who each bear a striking resemblance to a lion, a man, a bull, and an eagle—angels who, say theologians, also correspond with each of the four Gospels, which in turn each represent one of four unique qualities of Jesus Christ.

What do have so far, then? Four tribes of Israel; four signs of The Zodiac; four Living Creatures; four Gospels; four qualities of Christ.

Put it all together, and what have we got?

We've got Matthew's Gospel of Christ as King corresponding with Judah's lion of Leo; Luke's Gospel of Christ as Son of Man corresponding with Reuben's man of Aquarius; Mark's Gospel of Christ as Servant corresponding with Ephraim's bull of Taurus; and John's Gospel of Christ as Son of God corresponding with Dan's eagle, or in this case, its enemy, the scorpion of Scorpio.

---

[68] *Numbers* 2:1-2

All in all, I'd say these interwoven strands of symbolism weave quite a remarkable tapestry that reveals just how The Zodiac really does "declare the glory of God."

Of course, there will be those who insist this correspondence is completely invalid on the grounds that the names and imagery of the constellations aren't biblical, citing the notion that they were handed down to those sixth-century Jews from the Greeks and Romans. However, I'd remind them that these details had actually been handed down long before that time. If you'll recall, Job was cited as already calling the constellations by their names—Orion, Arcturus, and the Pleiades—at a time that predated the Greeks and Romans by more than five centuries.

So from whom did Job receive this knowledge of the names of the constellations? As it so happens, he received it from a book written by a man *The Bible* says walked and talked with God. That man was Enoch; and from his conversation with God, we learn some things very pertinent to our discussion. Said Enoch:

> And now, my children, I know all things, because I heard it from the Lord Himself, and have seen it with my own eyes...
>
> What I learned, I wrote in books... I measured and described the stars—a countless multitude.
>
> Who knows their revolutions and which direction they're going? Not even the angels know how many there are, but I've written down the names of them all.[69]

So much for the alleged original contribution of the Greeks and Romans. Compared to Enoch, they're Johnny-come-latelies.

Now, in looking at The Zodiac in a way that most Christians rarely if ever do, our next stop involves a similar activity. We'll next be looking at The Sphinx and The Great Pyramid of Giza.

Certainly most everyone is familiar with the Sphinx of Egypt. But what most aren't aware of is the Great Sphinx isn't just one megalith among several located in the Giza Pyramid Complex. It's also a symbol of great significance at such sacred sites as the Temple of Esneh, in Upper Egypt.

In his book, *The Witness of the Stars*, E.W. Bullinger says that painted on the ceiling of the Temple of Esneh is something known as The Denderah Zodiac. Unlike most images of The Zodiac, though, this one contains an unusual feature: This Zodiac includes the tiny image of the Sphinx—an image that just happens to be located between Virgo the Virgin, and Leo the Lion. According to Bullinger, the word *sphinx*

---

[69] *The Secrets of Enoch* 40:1-4

means to "bind together." Taking this meaning, then, together with the location of this image of the Sphinx, Bullinger believes the Denderah Zodiac is revealing something our modern Zodiac, which begins with Aries the Ram, no longer reveals. It's telling us that The Zodiac should begin with Virgo and end with Leo. In short, the real message contained in The Zodiac is the story of Christ, in terms of the dual aspects of His Coming to Earth. First, He came by way of the virgin of Bethlehem, as the suffering servant of God, typified by Virgo, and second, by way of the lion of Judah, as the righteous instrument of God's wrath, typified by Leo.

In this, we again discover an uncanny correspondence between the gospel in the stars and the gospel in the written word.

One final piece to add to the puzzle: Job said, "By His Spirit, God has garnished the Heavens; His hand has formed the crooked serpent."[70] According to biblical scholars like Bullinger, among the few who've dared to speak out on this subject, we're told that Job was referring to the constellation of Draco the Dragon, a constellation so immense that it stretches across *a third of the expanse* of the night sky. How interesting, then, that John the Revelator said:

> Another sign appeared in Heaven, and look, a great fiery red dragon ... and with his tail, he drew *a third of the stars* of Heaven and threw them down to Earth.[71]

What's more, this constellation of Draco was well known in ancient times to have contained a star called Thuban, which, between four and six thousand years ago, was famous for being our North Star. Little wonder that this Dragon Star was used by the builders of The Great Pyramid of Giza to orient its entranceway to true north. In making this choice, the architect is said to be conveying the message that, prior to God's salvation effort via the death and resurrection of Christ, humanity was utterly dominated by Satan's influence, which is typified by the downward slope of the passage.

In view of such an avalanche of provocative connections, we can't help but wonder: How could such a remarkable aspect of God's revelation become obscured by such a dense cloud of suspicion? Just try naming another arena of life that reveals more about God's power than His communicating a universal message of redemption to an onlooking world.

Considering the importance of such a message, what greater enemy could there be to the powers of darkness, which is to say, the

---

[70] *Job* 26:13

[71] *Revelation* 12:3-4

devil and his minions? What could be more important to these powers than to do all they can to distort and confuse this message of the glory of God, declared from Heaven itself?

I guess when you look at it that way one of the greatest mysteries in God's creation doesn't seem so mysterious after all, now does it?

Misconception #41

*Jesus was Just a Poor Carpenter's Son
Before His Real Ministry Began*

EVERYONE LOVES a good "rags to riches" story, so what better way to attract attention to the life of Jesus than by plugging His story into this tried-and-true plotline. You know the sort of thing: Local boy makes good in spite of the odds against him; down-and-out-but-lovable oaf rises to the top of his game; so on and so forth.

In this case, our story runs as follows: Jesus of Nazareth was soon to be born into a poor, humble family that was desperately searching for a place to give birth to their first child. Eventually, they wound up, starving and cold, in a manger, where their baby was born alongside an odd assortment of scruffy farm animals. Fortunately for them, however, they received some much-needed handouts from another group of wanderers, a trio of Wise Men, who offered gifts of gold, frankincense, and myrrh.

In time—so the story continues—the child grew up and followed in the footsteps of his aged father, becoming a carpenter, with the two of them eking out a living as merely adequate woodworkers. Eventually, Joseph died and left the family business to Jesus, which He continued to run until His fateful encounter with His cousin, John the Baptist, who then anointed the lowly carpenter as the newly instated king of Israel.

Now that's what I call a story arc! Even Hollywood couldn't dream up one to beat that.

But tell me: Do you think a plotline as dramatic as that is really in *The Bible*? Sad to say, you can look all you want, but it just isn't there.

To which the rabid believers vehemently howl in protest: "How dare you question the Holy Scriptures!"

In my defense, though, as I've consistently done to this point, I'm not questioning *The Bible* itself. I'm questioning a watered-down version of it—courtesy of the three laws of disinformation. Now, I do admit, core elements of the plot can be found within the pages of Holy Writ, but unfortunately, the rest of the story as we've come to remember it has been embellished for dramatic effect.

How, then, do we dissect the truth from the embellishments in order to rescue the reality of what the Scriptures say about the life of Christ? Fortunately, the answer, as usual, lies in a thorough examination of what *The Bible* says in terms of its original language and context. In other words, to get at the truth, we first accurately translate the passages that speak of the pertinent aspects of Jesus' life, and then we restore the story to its original form. Here we go, then.

The second chapter of *The Gospel of Luke* records that Joseph and Mary were responding to a decree of Augustus Caesar, which ordered everyone living in the Roman territories to go to the birthplace of their family and pay their taxes. And because Joseph and Mary were both descendants of King David, they went to Bethlehem to perform their duties as tax-paying citizens. There, Mary came to term with their child, and trying to rent a room for the evening in a local inn, they were turned away, only to find refuge in a nearby stable.[72] It was not until sometime later—as Matthew described Jesus as being a young child by then—that the Three Wise Men, seeking the king of the Jews, arrived to deliver their birthday gifts.[73]

In time, the boy Jesus grew up, and like most sons at that time He followed in the footsteps of His elderly father, apprenticing in the family business. In this more-accurate version, though, Joseph wasn't a simple woodworker, because, in fact, wood was a rare commodity in a desert landscape like Palestine. As it so happens, the Greek word used in *Matthew* 13 and *Mark* 6 for "carpenter," which is *tekton*, can just as easily be translated as "architect" or "master builder." What this means is, a *tekton* is someone who's not only skilled in making furniture but houses and temples, too. And because wood was so scarce in that part of the country, this meant that a master builder would've more often than not been working with stone, as would a mason.

Then, upon the death of His father, Jesus wasn't left to His own devices for very long, because soon afterward, His great uncle—His mother Mary's uncle, actually—Joseph of Arimathea, took Him under his wing.

According to many historical accounts, this Joseph was by no means a poor man himself, having established quite a reputation as a merchant of precious metals. It's well known that Uncle Joseph and his royal nephew spent much of their time sailing up and down the frontier coastlands between Palestine and the British Isles. This was the period of Jesus' life referred to as "the lost years," that time from the age of twelve, when He astounded everyone in the Temple, to the age of thirty, when He reappeared to be baptized by John in the Jordan

---

[72] *Luke* 2:1-7

[73] *Matthew* 2:1-12

River. It was during those formative years that Jesus, like Moses before Him, was a man-in-training, in this case, traveling with his influential uncle. To this day, Britons still sing of Joseph, the tin merchant, of Jesus walking on England's pleasant pastures, and of the legendary deeds of that famous duo.

With all the preceding in mind, then, several things immediately jump out at us. First, if Joseph, the father of Jesus, had been a poor man, as tradition portrays him, he certainly wouldn't have bothered to journey, with his wife about to give birth, all the way to Bethlehem just to pay taxes. A poor man wouldn't worry about his little pittance of a tax payment, knowing full well it wouldn't be missed. Only a wealthy man would've expected his absence to be noticed at tax time—something that also explains why he tried to rent a room at the inn. That none were available speaks more to the fact that everyone was in town during the busy tax season, as opposed to their family being too poor to afford such a luxury. If they'd been as destitute as tradition has them, they would've simply set up camp in the first available location rather than try to rent a room for the night.

Similarly, the arrival of the Three Wise Men testified to another fact concerning the elevated status of Joseph and his family: Not only were they rich, but they were also born of royal blood. How odd that most people who assume Jesus and His parents were poor vagabonds neglect the details provided by Scripture confirming this. The Wise Men went first to Herod announcing they were looking for the Child Who they thought would be the next king of the Jews.[74] And they weren't the only ones who knew about the prophecy of His birth. When Herod questioned his own wise men about where this Child was supposed to be born, they told him, quite matter-of-factly:

> In Bethlehem of Judah—as it is written by the prophet: And you Bethlehem, in the land of Judah, who is the least among the princes of Judah, out of you will come a Governor Who will rule My people Israel.[75]

So, far from being considered a pauper's son, Jesus, right from the start, was known to have been born into a family of considerable note. Only centuries of disinformation, wrought by revisionist historians in some misguided attempt to make a good story even better, have muddied the waters.

Next comes the legend that reduced Jesus to the status of a mere carpenter. Again, we're confronted by the same forces that try to

---

[74] *Matthew* 2:1-16

[75] Ibid. 2:5-6

persuade us that Jesus was born into a poor, lowly family.

After all, what makes a better story than that? I mean, if Abraham Lincoln can go from reading by candlelight in a log cabin to the highest office in the land, then why can't our Lord and Savior go from lying in a manger to the throne of Heaven? Now that's what I call living the American Dream.

If Jesus were portrayed as a simple woodworker, then His rise to power would seem all the more miraculous, wouldn't it? Never mind that Jesus spoke less of His work as a carpenter, choosing instead to emphasize His role as a master builder and stonemason. Never mind about what He told us in *The Gospel of Matthew*.

> "Have you never read in the Scriptures," asked Jesus, "that the Stone which the builders rejected, the same has become the Chief Cornerstone? This is the Lord's doing, and it's marvelous in our eyes!
>
> And whoever falls on this Stone shall be broken, and on whomever it falls, it will grind them to powder."[76]

And again:

> When Jesus departed the Temple, His disciples came to ask Him about its structure. And Jesus said to them: "Do you see all this? I'm telling you, here and now, there won't be a single stone used to build this place that won't eventually be torn down."[77]

Then, as if to confirm His preoccupation with stonework, Luke recorded his own take on the subject.

> And when the crowds saw Jesus coming their way, they sang out their praises, but the Pharisees amongst the group told Him to rebuke them. To which Jesus replied that if they did hold back their adulation even the stones would cry out their praise to Him.[78]

Some scholars believe that Jesus wasn't speaking of some random pile of stones lying about the road somewhere, but that He was actually speaking—though in veiled terms—of the greatest megalithic monument ever built. The stones He was talking about were the ones used to construct The Great Pyramid of Giza, which has been demonstrated—via more than three and a half centuries of

---

[76] *Matthew* 21:42-44

[77] Ibid. 24:1-2

[78] *Luke* 19:37-40

scholarship—to contain a biblically-inspired timeline of prophetic history. Said Joseph A. Seiss: "The numerical values ... in the dimensions of The Great Pyramid's construction, with its geometric proportions ... speak as loudly as stones can be made to speak."

Then, immediately following Jesus' comments about these stones, Luke continued:

> So when Jesus approached the city, He mourned over it and its inhabitants, because the things that God had prepared for it as an offering of peace were instead hidden from it, because He knew the days were coming when its enemies would encircle the city and destroy it. And because of their ignorance as to the day of visitation from God, every stone in the city would be torn down to the ground."[79]

A Chief Cornerstone, a Temple made of stone, stones that cry out their praise to the Savior, and stones of a city torn down in the day of visitation. For someone who was supposedly a carpenter's son, Jesus sure didn't have much to say about wood; obviously, the Man Who was the Chief Cornerstone Himself was all about stone.

Finally, as for the period of Jesus' life when He was traveling under the tutelage of His great uncle Joseph, we should consider the numerous accounts of His exploits, not as a poor woodworker but as a master builder and architect. The traditions of Glastonbury tell of one such account to this day: Not only did Jesus build the first church on English soil with His own hands, in honor of His mother Mary, but He also designed it Himself—something He could never have done had He been a mere carpenter's son.

How sad to that think the truth of *The Bible* can be lost or obscured this way because prevailing attitudes so easily distort its original meaning. Yet, how fortunate that, with some investigative work, we're able to counteract the effects of the three laws of disinformation. Whenever they manage to blot out the truth, we only need to persist in ferreting out the facts, and eventually, what we uncover washes away all the distortions. And in the end, in spite of the lure of a good yarn, the truth is still far more exhilarating and edifying than any embellishments we face, no matter how well intentioned they might be.

---

[79] *Luke* 19:41-44

Misconception #40

Mary the Mother of Jesus was Born Via a Virgin Birth Just Like Her Son

WE DECLARE: "I believe in Jesus Christ, God's only Son, our Lord, Who was conceived by the Holy Spirit and born of the Virgin Mary. Jesus suffered under Pontius Pilate and was crucified; He died and was buried. He descended to the dead; on the third day He rose again; and He ascended to Heaven. Now He is seated at the right hand of the Father, and He will come to judge the living and the dead."

This excerpt, which describes Jesus' role in the salvation of humanity, comes to us from the Apostles' Creed, a statement of faith that expresses the core elements of what we believe to be true of the Gospel of Christ. All agree, for example, that Jesus was born of the Virgin Mary—Catholics and non-Catholics alike. Because God demanded a perfect sacrifice to satisfy the requirements of the Law, Jesus, as the Lamb of God, had to be perfect in all His ways, from the moment He was born till the moment He died. It also demanded, say theologians, that He be born without sin—thus the virgin birth was required to guarantee Christ's absolute perfection.

But what we don't all agree on is the issue of whether or not Mary herself was also born as the result of a virgin birth. Catholics say she was; non-Catholics say she wasn't. And the first thing critics of the virgin birth of Mary point to is the Apostles' Creed, which was approved by the Catholic Church in the fourth century. It states that Jesus was born of a virgin; however, any mention of Mary having been born in a similar way is clearly absent.

So, if Catholic doctrine in the fourth century didn't include the belief that Mary had been born of a virgin, when did it start and why?

According to most church historians, the idea that Mary was born of a virgin didn't begin to surface until more than a hundred years after the establishment of the Apostles' Creed. Officially dubbed the "immaculate conception," the idea is said to have originated sometime between the fifth and seventh centuries, as more and more people were becoming convinced that in order to conceive the sinless Son of God,

Mary herself must have been sinless, too. But to be sinless like Jesus, it wasn't enough that she be free from sin during her lifetime; it also required that she be born of a virgin like Jesus. And thus, Mary was elevated to just such a status.

So, regardless of whether you accept any of this about Mary's origins, this is the way most historians explain how the idea of her virgin birth developed.

But is that all there is to the story? Could a belief like this really materialize out of thin air just because well-intentioned believers required it?

Frankly, no, I don't think so. It's not the whole story; and I certainly don't believe an idea like this could've just appeared out of nowhere, either. Again and again throughout this list, what we've seen is, great misconceptions always take hold as a direct result of their being founded on a solid foundation of scriptural truth.

The question that remains, then, is: Which book of *The Bible* does it come from? There's nothing in the canonical record that suggests that Mary was anything more than an ordinary human being. Saintly? Yes. Blessed above all women? Absolutely. Born of a virgin like Jesus? Hardly.

And believe me: I'm not saying this because I don't love Mary with all my heart. I thank the Lord above for what she did for us. What she went through, in being the mother of Jesus, is beyond belief. Facing the dilemma of being pregnant while still only engaged, and having to tell Joseph about it. Knowing she'd given birth to the most special child in the world, yet having to face all the unknown factors that that high privilege forced upon her. Watching the life and death of her Son unfold before her in all its bittersweet irony.

Jesus was all her Son, yet all God's Son. Though she suckled Him and raised Him, she was at times spurned by Him. As a child, Jesus wandered off by Himself, and only later did Mary and Joseph find Him at the Temple. Imagine, then, her sadness when, even at the age of twelve, He was already distancing Himself from her. "Why are you looking for Me?" He asked His parents. "Don't you know I have to take care of My Father's business?"[80]

Then, when her Son had grown to manhood, Mary had wished to speak with Him, so Jesus' disciples told Him that His mother was outside their tent looking for Him. Again, we can only imagine how she felt when she heard His reply—not brought to her personally but by someone else. His response: "Who's My mother?"[81]

---

[80] *Luke* 2:49

[81] *Matthew* 12:49

And still later, when Jesus was betrayed and all His followers fled the scene in terror, she didn't abandon Him. Watching Him hang on the cross—scorned, rejected, an object of revulsion—she stood with Him until the end.

So, do I admire her? Yes. Do I love her? Absolutely. Do I worship her because I think she was born of a virgin like Jesus? Hardly. I don't worship her because the Lord tells us to have no other God but Him. And I don't think she was born of a virgin because there's nothing in *The Bible* that tells me she was.

However, just because I don't worship Mary doesn't mean I don't love her any less. Just because I don't think she was born of a virgin doesn't mean I don't admire her any less for what she did, in bearing and raising Jesus, and enduring all she suffered because of her undying loyalty to Him.

So, having ruled out the canonical record as a potential source for the idea that Mary was born of a virgin, where might it have come from?

As it turns out, it originated from a source we've already encountered several times in previous essays. I'm talking about the less-familiar passages of the apocryphal literature—in this case, in two texts of what's known as *The Lost Books of The Bible*. The first book we'll look at, appropriately enough, is called *The Gospel of the Birth of Mary*. And whether or not you choose to accept its inspiration as being of divine origin, one thing seems beyond question. When you read what it says, in the context of this issue of Mary's unique birth, you can't help but be intrigued at the possibility that this one little book did in fact influence a great many people who accepted its authenticity.

In *The Gospel of the Birth of Mary*, we find that Mary's parents were named Joachim and Anna, both of whom had sprung from the royal lineage of King David. Mary's father was a Galilean from Nazareth; her mother, from Bethlehem. Devoted members to the local Temple, they lived humbly in the sight of God, esteemed by everyone; yet for twenty years they remained childless.[82]

In time, although Joachim and his wife continually brought their offerings to the Temple, the townspeople began to question the efficacy of those offerings because they were still childless, citing the Scripture: "Cursed is everyone who doesn't give birth to a male child in Israel." So, to remove himself from the shame of his family's predicament, Joachim retired from the service of the Temple and went to work in the fields as a shepherd.[83]

---

[82] *The Gospel of the Birth of Mary* 1:2-5

[83] *The Gospel of the Birth of Mary* 1:7-12

Sometime later, while Joachim was tending his flock, an angel appeared before him and said:

> God wants you to know, Joachim, that He's seen how you've been unjustly treated for being childless. And because He's received your prayers and offerings, He sent me to tell you His purpose in all of this. Sometimes, when God shuts the womb of a woman, He has a special purpose in mind. He does it so He can open it again in an even more profound way. That way, such a birth won't be seen as being a product of mere desire but as a gift from God.
>
> Just look at the mother of your nation, Sarah: She was barren until later in her life, yet, even at her age, she brought forth Isaac, whose promised birth was a blessing to the nations.
>
> The same thing happened to Rachel, who was such a favorite of God and so loved by Jacob; even she continued barren for many years before she gave birth to Joseph, who not only governed Egypt but also delivered many nations from perishing from hunger.
>
> And who among the judges was braver than Samson or more devout than Samuel; yet both of their mothers were considered barren for a long time.
>
> In the same way, then, your wife Anna will conceive in her advanced years and will provide you with a daughter that you'll name Mary. According to your own vow, she'll be devoted to the Lord from her infancy, being filled with the Holy Spirit from her mother's womb...
>
> And in time, just as she was uniquely born of one who was barren, so she will in an unparalleled manner—while yet a virgin—bring forth the Son of the Most High. He'll be called Jesus, and according to the significance of His Name, He'll be the Savior of the world.[84]

How interesting is that? And how strange to think that such a controversial misconception as this, so divisive in the history of two great streams of the Christian Church, could actually have its roots in the scriptural record, after all.

And not only can this story be found in *The Gospel of the Birth of Mary*, but it can also be found in the very next text of *The Lost Books of The Bible*, called *The Protevangelion*, otherwise known as *An Historical Account of the Birth of Christ*, said to be written by James the Lesser, the

---

[84] Ibid. 2:1-10, 12

half-brother of Jesus.

In *The Protevangelion*, James records his own version of the same events. According to him, the high priest barred Joachim from presenting any more offerings at the Temple, citing that it was illegal for him to do so because he was an Israelite with no children. Joachim was so embarrassed he fled to the wilderness without even telling his wife where he'd gone. And there he remained in prayer for several weeks, having determined in his heart that he wouldn't go home until God had delivered him from his predicament.[85]

With no idea where her husband had disappeared to or why, a grief-stricken Anna took refuge in her garden, wearing her wedding dress, and there, under a laurel tree, she tearfully begged God to hear her prayers just as He'd heard Sarah's so long ago and blessed her with the birth of Isaac.[86]

Soon afterward, an angel came to Anna and told her, "The Lord has heard your prayer, and you'll conceive and give birth to a child who'll be spoken of throughout the whole world."[87]

Likewise, an angel appeared to Joachim with the good news of the impending birth of his child, and returning home, he was reunited with his wife once again.[88] And the rest, as they say, is history.

So, not only does this story of Mary's unique birth appear in the apocryphal record, but it appears there twice—back-to-back—as it is written: In the mouth of two or three witnesses, a thing is confirmed.[89]

No wonder the hearts and minds of the people have for all these centuries been so willing to embrace the idea that Mary, like her Son, was born in a miraculous manner. Even when many of the early Church Fathers tried to discredit and expunge such accounts from the official record, their influence remained indelibly etched in the memory traces of humanity.

Now that we've examined what the apocryphal literature says about the peculiar circumstances of Mary's birth, let's return to the canonical record to see what else it says. And although *The New Testament* doesn't provide anywhere near the level of detail that the apocryphal record does, one thing is clear: Nowhere in it is a shred of evidence that suggests Jesus ever saw Mary as being anything more than an ordinary human being. Not only that, but according to the

---

[85] *Protevangelion* 1:1-2, 6-7

[86] Ibid. 1:1-2, 8-10

[87] Ibid. 4:1

[88] Ibid. 4:4

[89] *Matthew* 18:16, *Second Corinthians* 13:1

gospel record, Jesus didn't even consider her to be any more important than anyone among His entourage.

> While Jesus continued to speak to the people, His mother and brothers stood outside, hoping to speak to Him.
> Then someone told Him: "Excuse me, Master, but Your mother and brothers are outside looking for You."
> But He just replied, quite matter-of-factly: "Who's My mother? And who are My brothers?" And gesturing to His disciples, He said, "See here, this is My mother, and these are My brothers. Whoever does the will of My Father in Heaven, the same is My brother and sister and mother."[90]

Then, echoing this same idea in his Gospel, Luke described the time when, as Jesus was speaking to a crowd of people, a woman said to Him:

> "Blessed is the woman who gave birth to You, and the breasts that You suckled upon."
> To which Jesus replied, "On the contrary, blessed are those who hear the words of God and do what they say."[91]

Now, I ask you: Does this sound as if Jesus wanted us to believe His mother was anything more than an ordinary human being, something that could never have been the case had she been born of a virgin herself?

Certainly, Jesus looked upon Mary as a God-ordained vessel; of that there's no question. However, just as certainly, He never intended that she be treated as being more exalted than Himself, something that Mary, to her everlasting credit, never once tried to instigate on her own behalf. To her dying day, she was content with simply being the human vessel that the Lord chose to flow through in the Incarnation.

And besides, what's so bad with the position in life *The Bible* portrays for Mary, anyway? Why is it so important that she be more than what she appears to be?

The obvious answer is: There is no reason. To be chosen to give birth to the Son of God while yet a virgin is certainly the most amazing thing that anyone has ever had the opportunity to do in the whole history of humanity. So why does anybody have to embellish it beyond that?

After all, in light of the apocryphal record, who could argue that Mary's birth was not among the most extraordinary births in human

---

[90] *Matthew* 12:46-50; *Mark* 3:31-35; *Luke* 8:21-22

[91] *Luke* 11: 27-28

history, apart from Christ's birth, naturally? But add to that the fact that Mary's life can lay claim to this connection between her special birth and her Son's undeniably places her at the pinnacle of human experience. And that is something that neither Protestants can erase nor Catholics can lose should the idea of Mary's so-called "immaculate conception" turn out to be merely an outgrowth of these apocryphal texts.

Either way you look at, though, as is so often the case when faced with the paradoxical nature of God's word, we're forced to accept that there's always more than one way to look at issues like this. And rather than assume that one position is all right and that therefore the other position is all wrong, maybe we should try instead to see this as though both sides are in touch with two equally valid aspects of the same truth.

In other words, if you're of the opinion held by Protestants, that Mary was a saintly woman blessed by the Holy Spirit to convey the mortal portion of God's immortality, then clearly there's a scriptural foundation for that view. But if you're of the opinion held by Catholics, that Mary was miraculously conceived to set her apart in giving birth to the divine Son of God in this sin-infested world, then you, too, can point to a scriptural foundation for that belief as well.

So, far from being divided on such a controversial issue, we can always turn to God's word, no matter how obscured by misuse, to find a common ground of truth, which oddly enough is just another way of saying that for once, as believers, even we can have our cake and eat it, too.

Misconception #39

When Jesus Commended a Person for Offering Water to the Least of His Brothers, He Meant It to Anyone in Need

IT'S TRUE: Everybody loves a good old-fashioned story of giving. Whether it's Santa Claus handing out his bag of goodies on Christmas Eve, or Robin Hood stealing from the rich and giving to the poor, we all love the idea of someone who gives their all to make other people better off. We can't help it; it makes us feel warm and fuzzy inside. That's how we are. After all, it's just as Jesus said: "It's more blessed to give than to receive."[92]

That's why this next misconception is so tricky to deal with.

In this case, what we're dealing with is a statement Jesus made, in which He seems to commend anyone who offers a cup of cold water to people in need. Almost everyone is aware of the story in one form or another; almost everyone has his or her own take on it. But what does *The Bible* really have to say about it? We find the most familiar rendition of this story in *The Gospel of Mark*.

One day, Jesus was teaching His disciples about His kingdom and the perils they'd have to endure to achieve His ultimate blessing. Then and there, He predicted His own impending death and resurrection, but they were too afraid to ask Him to explain what He was talking about. Confused, they were all too preoccupied with their own worries. Less concerned about the trials and tribulations that came with being associated with Jesus, they were more interested in finding out who among them was going to be the greatest in His kingdom. But when Jesus asked them what they'd been quarreling about, the disciples were too embarrassed to admit what they'd been discussing. So Jesus proceeded to explain to them that anyone who wanted to be first in His kingdom would have to be last, and a servant to everyone.

Impetuous as ever, though, the disciples kept on griping, as they told Jesus about a stranger who they'd seen casting out demons in His Name. But because they didn't know the man, they explained that they'd forbidden him to continue what he was doing. Jesus then replied that they should never hinder anyone in such activities. No one

---

[92] *Acts* 20:35

performing such miracles could ever be accused of doing evil, because whoever wasn't against Him was really on His side. And as if to punctuate what He was saying, He made one of His most famous pronouncements: "And whoever gives you a cup of cold water in My Name, because you belong to Christ, will certainly receive his reward for doing so."[93]

What, then, does this story seem to be teaching us?

On the surface, it seems as though Jesus is saying that you should always be willing to lend a helping hand to those in need, as though handing out a cup of cold water to anyone is to be commended. Accordingly, the Lord has always been portrayed as being more concerned with the giver than the receiver; at least that's what this rendition of the story would have us believe.

But remember, as we've discussed at length in previous essays, the apparent truth is often a prisoner of the context in which it's presented. This is where tradition is such a hindrance to what *The Bible* is really trying to communicate, because Jesus doesn't just talk about this subject in Mark's Gospel. He also talks about it, in a much broader context, in Matthew's Gospel.

"But why," you may ask, "am I making such a fuss? What's wrong with the story the way we've been interpreting it all these years? Jesus is commending people who give good things to anyone in need; how can you improve a message like that? And why would you want to, anyway?"

Turns out, it's important because the message of giving in *The Bible* is so important. Turns out, it's not good enough that Jesus commend somebody for some indiscriminate act, no matter how well intentioned it may seem, because with God, it's not the act that counts but the motive.

Just think: How many times in Scripture have you seen God and Jesus condemn some apparently "holy" activity because they saw that the motive behind the action betrayed the spiritual dimension of the act? For example, people who prayed on a street corner were condemned because they didn't care if God heard them, they just wanted everyone to see them praying; and those who gave their offerings at the Temple were condemned because they didn't care about mercy or justice, they were just trying to bribe God into helping them. All this to say, because proper giving is so central to the heart of God, every Christian should strive to find out what it is about a person's giving that causes Jesus to memorialize them and their action. With that in mind, let's look at this story in light of Matthew's Gospel,

---

[93] *Mark* 9:31-41

which encompasses the entire tenth chapter.

Jesus sent His twelve disciples out amongst the people, where they were to proclaim that the Kingdom of Heaven was manifesting itself in their very midst. Wherever they went, they were to invoke His Name—to heal the sick, to cast out demons, and to raise the dead. All this they were to do, but on one condition: They weren't allowed to take any money with them on their journey, explaining that as "workers in the field," as it were, they were worthy of their hire.

They were to travel from city to city, and wherever they went, they were to be provided for; and whoever declined to do so would bear the responsibility for their actions—or to be more precise in this case, their failure to act. As sheep amongst wolves, Jesus sent them into the harvest field, admonishing them to be harmless as doves but wise as serpents. Warning them about the perils they'd face for His sake, He yet assured them that they'd be divinely guided by the Spirit of God in all that they'd face. Hatred, persecution, and death would be their lot, but whoever endured would be saved in the end. They were told in no uncertain terms that their enemies would be among their own household, and that if any of them loved their families more than Him they weren't worthy of Him. They were told simply to take up their crosses and follow Him. Whoever found his life would lose it, and whoever lost his life for Christ's sake would find it.[94]

What's more, whoever received them would be receiving Christ, and whoever received Him would, in fact, be receiving the One Who'd sent Him, because He said:

> Anyone receiving a prophet in the name of a prophet receives a prophet's reward, and anyone receiving a righteous man receives a righteous man's reward.
>
> And whoever gives one of these special ones a cup of cold water, in the name of a disciple, I tell you here and now they'll certainly be rewarded for it.[95]

We can see, then, how the context of this chapter provides a completely new view of the verses in question. Far from conveying the idea that Jesus intends to bless just anyone who passes out indiscriminate cups of water, we see what centuries of disinformation have obscured. Having restored what's been lost for so long, we see a simple yet powerful truth so important to the heart of God.

The ones Jesus intends to reward are those who provide for those He's commissioned to bring the Good News of the Gospel to the whole

---

[94] *Matthew* 10:1-39

[95] Ibid. 10:40-42

world. Those kind of people, and only those kind, should ever expect to receive the blessing that Jesus speaks of here; and we should therefore do away with the notion that the Lord is in any other business than to sustain the workers of His harvest. To believe otherwise would be a disservice to Christ, Who knew exactly what He was doing when He ordained and sent out His disciples, as sheep amongst wolves, in a world fraught with danger on every side.

So, in reviewing the entire tenth chapter of *Matthew*, instead of focusing on just one verse, we can't help but better understand what Jesus was really thinking when He offered His famous commendation. To those bringing the water of God's word, water should be given; to those bringing the sustenance of God's promise, sustenance should be given. And in so doing, a marvelous balance of life would ensue: Both the heart of humanity and the heart of God would be satisfied.

But to those who refuse to participate in this divine dance, their portion only brings sorrow. Not only to them, though, but to the Lord also, just as when Jesus gazed out over His beloved but rebellious city of Jerusalem, of whom it was said: "He came to His own, but His own received Him not."[96] As He looked, He could not help but weep bitterly, because He knew all too well of those dark days ahead when His people would finally cry out in genuine gratitude: "Blessed are those who come in the Name of the Lord."[97]

---

[96] *John* 1:11
[97] *Matthew* 23:37-39

Misconception #38

When Jesus' Listeners Demanded a Sign, He Told Them No More Signs from God Would be Given

ONCE UPON A TIME God was in the business of providing signs and wonders to His people in an ongoing effort to lead them through life's struggle. Ten plagues struck Egypt and the Red Sea parted at the command of Moses, the Sun stood still in the sky at the behest of Joshua, and a widow's son was raised from the dead at the order of Elijah. An iron axe-head floated for Elisha, a donkey talked to Balaam, and three Hebrew children survived after having been thrown into a fiery furnace.

From beginning to end, in fact, *The Bible* is nothing if not a litany of signs and wonders.

Yet one day, God decided to stop providing these marvelous indicators of His divine guidance, choosing instead to leave humanity to fend for itself ever after. Even more mind-boggling than the miracles themselves: It's said that God ceased these divine intrusions into history with the arrival of the greatest miracle worker of all time, Jesus Christ.

As it so happened, Jesus had been in the habit of going about healing everyone He met, when He'd come upon a man who was possessed by a demon. Although the man was blind and mute because of this demon, he suddenly found himself completely healthy again in the presence of Jesus.

Amazed, someone in the crowd asked: "How can this be? Isn't this Jesus just a son of David?"

And when the Pharisees heard about it, they said Jesus was casting out demons with the power of Beelzebub, the prince of demons.[98]

To which Jesus replied:

> But don't you realize that every kingdom divided will be destroyed, and every house divided can never stand. If Satan casts out Satan, then he's divided against himself. How will a kingdom like that ever hope to remain strong? And if I cast out demons with the help of Beelzebub, then by what power do

---

[98] *Matthew* 12:22-24

your children cast them out? Therefore, they'll be your judges. But on the other hand, if I cast out demons by the Spirit of God, then the Kingdom of God has come upon you.[99]

Then, some of the scribes and Pharisees responded to this display of power by insisting: "Teacher, we want you to give us a sign."[100]

But Jesus answered:

> Only an evil and adulterous generation goes about craving signs. But I'm telling you: No sign will be given to it but the sign of the prophet Jonah, because as Jonah was in the belly of the whale for three days and nights, so also the Son of Man will be three days and nights in the heart of the Earth.
>
> Then the men of Nineveh will rise in judgment against this generation to condemn it, because they repented at the preaching of Jonah. But see how someone even greater than Jonah is here.[101]

Add to that, the Apostle Mark's take, and it pretty much seals the deal:

> When the Pharisees came forward, they began to tempt Jesus, demanding a sign from Heaven.
>
> Sighing deeply, Jesus said, "Why is this generation so eager for signs? But I'm telling you: There will be no signs given to it."
>
> And He left them, getting into a ship and departing to the other side of the lake.[102]

So there you have it: Jesus seemed quite emphatic, didn't He? Once and for all, He denied humanity the hope of ever receiving any more signs and wonders from His Father in Heaven. Isn't that how the text reads to you? It is, after all, how centuries of church tradition have interpreted it; and who's going to argue with that?

But wait; not so fast. Are you really so sure this is the last word on the subject? Yes, tradition may tell us it is, but as we've seen throughout this list, just because it insists Scripture says something doesn't always mean tradition is right. Unless further analysis of the rest of the book supports a particular view, we as believers need not and should not feel obligated to accept it, regardless of the weight of tradition.

---

[99] *Matthew* 12:25-28
[100] Ibid. 12:38
[101] Ibid. 12:39-41
[102] *Mark* 8:11-13

So what does the rest of *The Bible* have to say about God's intent to provide signs and wonders to humanity?

First, just for the sake of argument, let's assume the traditional reading of these passages is true. Let's say Jesus actually told us that—except for Jonah in that whale—we won't be receiving any more signs from the Lord. Then *The Bible*, as it continues its narrative from that point onward, should confirm this view, right?

So what do we see?

Well, according to Matthew, no sooner had Jesus ended His discussion with the scribes and Pharisees than He was feeding five thousand people—not counting their wives and children—with five loaves of bread and two fish.[103]

Then, immediately after that, Jesus had all His disciples get into a boat and sail ahead of Him to the other side while He went off to a nearby mountainside to pray by Himself.

All night the disciples were out on that boat, trying to make their way to the other side, but because the wind and the waves beat against them with such force, they never did quite make it there.

Then, just before dawn, the wind and the waves began to batter their boat with even greater intensity. As darkness slowly gave way to morning's first light, several of the weary disciples rubbed their eyes in disbelief: A mysterious figure was walking toward them, across the surface of the lake, even as the foamy spray of the waves enveloped it.

"My God, it's a ghost!" cried one of the disciples.

As the figure made its way to the edge of their boat, a familiar voice sliced through the din of wind and waves. "Don't worry, everyone; it's just Me."[104] Jesus, of course, walking on water—which if I'm not entirely mistaken was, like the feeding of the five thousand, a miracle.

On and on I could go: The blind saw, the lame walked, the deaf heard, the dead rose. One can only wonder what Lazarus would've thought had he ever heard someone tell him that God had stopped giving any more signs after Jonah's day.

"Well, Jesus may have performed plenty of miracles in His day," believers in the God of No More Signs might say, "but that doesn't mean there've been any since He rose from the dead and ascended to Heaven."

To which I'd reply, "Oh, really? What about all the signs Matthew talked about in his Gospel? You know, the ones Jesus predicted would take place in the Last Days? Don't those count?"

Jesus' disciples asked Him: "What will the signs of Your coming

---

[103] *Matthew* 14:15-21

[104] Ibid. 14:22-27

be like?"

And rather than tell them no more signs would be given to humanity, Jesus described a great many that would occur someday.

> Immediately after the tribulation of those days, the Sun will grow dark, the Moon will withhold her light, and even the stars will begin to fall from the sky. It'll be as if the very power of Heaven is being shaken. Then the sign of the Son of Man will appear in Heaven, and every tribe of the Earth will mourn, as they all see the Son of Man coming in the clouds with great power and glory.[105]

Not only did Matthew describe a litany of signs, but Luke also had Jesus predicting much of the same in his Gospel.

> Nation will rise against nation, and kingdom against kingdom. There will also be terrible earthquakes, famines, and pestilences in many places; and dreadful sights and great signs will appear from Heaven.[106]

Then, of course, there's *The Book of Revelation*, which is nothing but a catalog of one amazing sign after another, all of which are events that clearly occur many centuries after Jesus performed His signs and wonder on Earth.

So, whether we're talking about signs in Jesus' day, or those that will occur in the future, it's quite apparent that God has never wavered in His desire to provide signs and wonders for humanity.

Why, then, does tradition have us thinking otherwise?

The answer, I believe, lies in the fact that we who are living in a modern age have such a difficult time accepting that the world is a place where the ordinary can co-exist with the extraordinary. Thanks to the advent of the scientific age, mankind has been able—to its own satisfaction, at least—to express the mysteries of the cosmos in terms of laws that explain the inexplicable. In previous ages, what had been described in magical terms is now in our modern era explained in mechanical terms, thereby eliminating any need for the miraculous, the fantastic, the irrational.

As a result, even the Church of the Living God has become inoculated with the belief that the intervention of divine power is unnecessary when explaining how the Universe works. So much so in fact that when confronted with the idea of signs and wonders even Christians find themselves incapable of reconciling their occurrence in

---

[105] *Matthew* 24:29-30

[106] *Luke* 21:10-11

a modern, mechanistic world.

Yet despite all this, anyone who reads *The Bible* discovers that Jesus never, as modern traditions have assumed, placed a limit on His willingness to provide signs of His power.

So, if the Scriptures as a whole leave us no doubt that God is still willing to provide signs and wonders, then what is it about Jesus' statement about Jonah and the whale that has us believing otherwise?

Let's review that passage again—this time in light of what the rest of Scripture says—and I think you'll see.

Speaking to the scribes and Pharisees, Jesus said:

> Only an evil and adulterous generation goes about craving signs. But I'm telling you: No sign will be given to it but the sign of the prophet Jonah, because as Jonah was in the belly of the whale for three days and nights, so also the Son of Man will be three days and nights in the heart of the Earth.[107]

Now that we have it clear in our minds that this was the same Man Who healed the sick, fed the multitudes, and walked on water, maybe now we'll hear Him say what we didn't hear Him say before. Maybe we'll finally notice that Jesus didn't say that no sign would be given—period; He didn't say that no sign would be given but the sign of Jonah—period. What He said was that no sign would be given but those that, like the sign of Jonah, reveal the true nature of the Risen One, Who survived His own harrowing ordeal of three days and nights in the grave, of which the belly of the whale was a type.

What all this means, then, is, it isn't enough that you witness miracles of healing, of loaves and fish, or even of Jesus walking on water, if you don't fully apprehend what all these events signify. That was, after all, the great tragedy of the scribes and Pharisees' response to hearing about Jesus' miracles. No doubt some of them had even seen a few with their own eyes, but still it wasn't enough. Still they demanded more, which is why Jesus then said what He said. Not because He planned to cease providing signs and wonder, but because He knew that without the eye of faith, even the miracle of Jonah having been spit out, alive and well, on those ancient shores of Nineveh was nothing more than a quaint fable that only the gullible would ever be expected to believe.

---

[107] *Matthew* 12:39

Misconception #37

Jesus was Born on December 25th

IT REALLY IS the most wonderful time of the year: Christmas. I love everything having to do with the theme and message of the yuletide season. But what I love most about Christmas is that it's the one time of the year I feel normal—as a Christian, I mean. It's the one time of year that, wherever I go, I'm surrounded by what's most important to me, what fills my heart with the greatest happiness.

Now, I know as Christians we have our Sundays to celebrate the Lord's Day, and we've got Easter Sunday to celebrate the Lord's resurrection; but there's one thing that Christmastime has that Sundays or Easters don't have. And, no, I'm not talking about the presents, or the Christmas tree, or the decorations, or the family gatherings, or the food. What Christmas has that no other Christian celebration has: Christmas carols—carols everywhere you go, carols for weeks on end.

Why is that so special?

Well, think about it: When you go to church, you hear songs that talk about God and Jesus, and they remind you of why you're a Christian; and that's a wonderful thing. The same thing happens on Easter Sunday. The only letdown is, when you leave church and return to the so-called "real world," you're right back to business as usual: The song has faded.

Not at Christmastime, though; then, every day, all day, for weeks at a time, the song continues.

Now, I'm not referring to songs about roasting chestnuts on an open fire, or riding in a one-horse open sleigh, or even Santa coming to town. That's all great, up to a point, of course. What I'm talking about—the thing that makes me feel, as I say, normal all Christmas long—are the songs that talk about the Birth of Christ. Those wondrous lyrics that light my soul on fire in ways that no sermon or book can do. I think you know the ones I'm talking about:

> Hark the herald angels sing; glory to the newborn King! Peace on Earth and mercy mild; God and sinners reconciled.

And:

Joy to the World, the Lord has come; Let Earth receive her King!

And finally, my favorite:

Mary, did you know that your baby boy would one day walk on water? Mary, did you know that your baby boy would save our sons and daughters?

Did you know that your baby boy has walked where angels trod? And when you kissed your little baby, you've kissed the face of God?

So, you see, that's why Christmas is the one time of year I feel normal. It's also why I must beg your indulgence when I'm forced to talk about not only the Birth of Christ itself but also when that birth occurred. I say that because, as anyone reading these essays knows, the only thing I love as much as Christmas is uncovering truth that's been obscured by human traditions, to demonstrate to a skeptical world that *The Bible* can be trusted. So whatever you do, please don't misinterpret the following discourse as an attack on what's certainly our most beloved holiday—mine included.

My mission is two-fold: First, I want to demonstrate that what the Scriptures say about the Birth of Christ are valid and therefore capable of standing up to any form of scrutiny. Second, I want to peel away any useless claptrap that even the most naïve of Christmas lovers has to admit has distorted the true meaning of this special holiday.

As usual, let's begin with what most traditions say about Christmas.

As the story goes, there once was a couple of wandering Jews—Joseph and Mary, by name—and as it so happened, Mary had conceived a child in a most unusual way, which is to say, without the aid of normal matrimonial procedure. Then, because winter was taking hold around them as the time drew near for Mary to give birth to their special baby, the couple was desperate to find a suitable place of refuge. Just in the nick of time, though, they found a cozy manger in Bethlehem, where Mary gave birth to Jesus, and where the Three Wise Men, guided by that famous Star, came to deliver their gifts of gold, frankincense, and myrrh.

Pretty cool story, huh? Unfortunately, the story as it stands has a number of problems in the telling of it.

But mind you, I won't be heard to say there's a problem with the facts of the virgin birth, or the divinity of the Christ Child, or the divine guidance of the Three Wise Men. No, that's not something I'd ever disagree with. What I will disagree with is the idea that anything in

Scripture requires that these events had to occur on December 25th. Even more disagreeable, anyone who insists they're required is actually playing into the hands of the very ones who are constantly trying to destroy our confidence in the credibility of *The Bible*.

After all, we're not just talking about trying to convince the unconvinced about what the Scriptures have to say about Christmas. What about all the children who are taught to believe what the Christmas story is said to convey? How do you feel when they start asking questions about the glaring contradictions in regard to the events as they supposedly occurred? Do you insist they believe in whatever you tell them simply because you believe that's how the story went? Persist in that sort of logic, and you run the risk of their no longer believing anything you tell them about *The Bible*.

So, instead of continuing to ignore the many discrepancies in the Christmas story, why not use the brain God gave us to ferret out the real truth and disregard the human traditions that Jesus Himself warned us about? As C.S. Lewis explained: When getting at the true meaning of Scripture, we need never overreact by "throwing the baby out with the bathwater." Instead of hiding our heads in the sand—or in this case, the snow—whenever we encounter a distortion of truth, let's be "wise as serpents." Otherwise, not only will our children be worse off for it but so will all mankind.

Therefore, let's examine this most famous of all stories in light of the three laws of disinformation, as I've dubbed them: Latch, isolate, and repeat.

First, we're confidently told that, even though the land was in the throes of winter, shepherds were still tending their flocks in the field when Jesus was born. Not only that, but when the Three Wise Men arrived, they came upon a serenely snowbound scene in which the infant Savior was lying in a manger, wrapped only in swaddling clothes.

Second, once this charming, wintry scene has been planted in our minds, we're dissuaded from searching anywhere else in Scripture concerning the events of Christ's Birth, as this would be a complete waste of our time. Why? Well, naturally, because matters of faith are beyond the average person's ability to comprehend.

And third, we'll have it repeated to us over and over again what the angel told those shepherds as they watched over their flocks on those snow-covered fields that frigid, fateful night:

> Don't be afraid, because we bring you good news that today a Savior is born in the city of David, Who is Christ the Lord.

And as proof of this, you'll find a babe wrapped in swaddling clothes, lying in a manger.[108]

A marvelous story to be sure, but again I ask: Should it be accepted as such just because centuries of tradition have led us to do so? I mean, really, shepherds happily tending their flocks in the snow? Wise Men traipsing about a frigid countryside? Skimpily wrapped infants lying in barnyard mangers in winter? Do these details really sound consistent with a snowbound scenario? Talk about "suspension of disbelief"—and on a global scale, no less.

Now, as I say, this doesn't mean I don't believe there were angels proclaiming good news to shepherds in their fields, or that there were Wise Men delivering their gifts to the newborn King in His manger. Naturally if I didn't believe any of that, I could hardly call myself a Christian. I'm simply saying it's time we put some real flesh-and-blood on this situation in order to finally grasp the truth of this moment that has for so long remained—dare I risk saying it?—frozen in time in the hearts and minds of so many faithful believers.

But before we can do that, we first must be willing to ask the hard questions: Why does it matter what time of year Jesus was born? Isn't it enough just to know He was born? And if it is so important to know, then why isn't there anything in *The Bible* to help us determine when His birth took place?

Granted, for many who believe in Jesus Christ, nothing anyone says or does will change how they feel. For them, the time of year He was born simply doesn't matter; all that concerns them is to know He was born, and so they're perfectly satisfied to leave it at that. But unfortunately, the flipside of that conviction is that being a Christian doesn't just involve believing what we believe for our own sakes and being done with it. It also involves having a responsibility to others—to ask ourselves how specific beliefs about God and Jesus relate to those around us. Consequently, we must face the fact that a great many people are confused by this debate. Many have come to a crossroad over this very issue, in which answers to questions about when Christ was born will inevitably lead them down one path or another.

And as these undecided ones stand at this crossroad, gazing up at the signs that aim them down various avenues, what do they see? The most obvious sign, of course, points to Jesus as being merely *a* savior among *dozens of other* saviors, all who are said to have died and risen again, and all—speaking directly to our present misconception—who are said to have been born on the 25th of December.

---

[108] *Luke* 2:8-12

For example, the Babylonians worshiped a heroic figure by the name of Tammuz, who was miraculously born of Semiramis, the wife of Nimrod. Now, when I say miraculous, I don't mean that Tammuz was born by way of a virgin—not even close, in fact, because clearly Semiramis had been married to Nimrod long before the birth of Tammuz. What we're talking about is a miracle in the following sense: Long after her husband had died, Semiramis found herself pregnant; and because Nimrod had been worshiped as a god, Semiramis, hoping to capitalize on this, came up with the inspired idea of claiming that Nimrod's soul had descended upon her in the form of a sunbeam and impregnated her. Thus, Tammuz was born, his "miraculous" birth equated ever after with the rebirth of the Sun, and so, too, was the legend of the Sun-god born, on ... you guessed it ... December 25th.

So powerful was this story of the rebirth of the Sun-god, which was clearly linked to the Winter Solstice that marked the shortest day of the year and the promised return of Spring, in no time a holiday observing the Sun's rebirth was being held throughout the ancient world. Among the various personifications of the Sun-god: Horus of Egypt, Mithra of Persia, Dionysus of Greece, and Bacchus of Rome—all supposedly born at this same time of the year, and all associated with legends that spoke of their having been resurrected from the dead.

It's this overabundance of messianic figures—insist detractors of Jesus as being the one and only true Savior—that demonstrates Christ is not unique among the pantheon of gods. "Jesus is not the Lord of all Creation," they say, "not the Child Who'd one day rule the nations." He's just the product of an overactive Jewish imagination, an amalgam of all the dying-and-rising saviors that came before Him. And the key to proving it: "Look," they say, "you're all celebrating His birthday on the same day as all these other god-men!"

For this reason, then, the issue of what time of year Jesus was born shifts from one in which we're defending a pleasant holiday, filled with fond memories of hearth and heart, to one in which we're now aiding and abetting those who seek to undermine the very foundation of the Christian faith. In other words, when Christians insist there's nothing wrong with celebrating Christmas on December 25th, they may just want to consider the possibility that in doing so they're allowing Jesus to be denigrated through an association with every other pseudo-savior who claims to be born on the same day.

"What do we do, then, to counteract this attack?" you might ask. "Do we stop celebrating Christmas on December 25th? Do we do away with Christmas altogether?"

"God forbid," I'd then reply.

"What? You mean you're not saying we have to get rid of the

Christmas trees, or the Christmas presents, or the Christmas carols?"

"Heavens, no; are you kidding? No, the carols stay. All of it stays—the trees, the presents, and most definitely the carols."

"What, then? How do we counteract the idea that Jesus is just another alleged savior born of December 25th?"

"Very simple, really: We demonstrate from Scripture the *actual* time of year Jesus was born, and when we do, the entire argument of the detractors folds like a house of cards."

"I don't get it. How does that solve the problem?"

"Well, think about it: What's the main argument of critics of *The Bible*? According to them, long before Jesus ever came onto the scene, there were all these other heroes who did all sorts of things that Jesus reportedly did—performing miracles, having twelve disciples, dying and resurrecting, ascending to Heaven, those sorts of things."

"Right; and their all being born on December 25th."

"That's right. And how do they explain how it happened? They say it was because whoever wrote *The New Testament* borrowed from all these past lives, wove them all together, and concocted the latest version of the dying-and-rising hero—this time, called Jesus Christ."

"So ... if you can show that *The Bible* has Jesus ... being born on some other day besides December 25th...?"

"Then the linchpin that holds together the argument that says the gospel writers lied about Jesus doing everything He did goes away, and down comes the cradle, baby and all."

"Ahhh, I get it, yeah. But I thought *The Bible* didn't tell us when Jesus was born; at least that's what I've been told."

"Well, if by that you mean it doesn't come right out and say Jesus was born on such and such date, no, it doesn't. But that doesn't mean there isn't a way to research events in Scripture to deduce the time of year Jesus was born, give or take a week or two."

So, yes, as it turns out, contrary to popular belief, the antidote to this whole dilemma lies simply in a willingness to look to what *The Bible* has declared all along, even as traditions have grown up as a hedge to deter anyone from looking for themselves.

Let's take some time, then, to examine the chronology of events as the Scriptures depict them, and you'll see what I'm talking about.

While three of the gospel writers skimmed past the details of Christ's birth, Luke did record them. Concerning the Lord's cousin, John the Baptist, he wrote:

> In the days of Herod, the king of Judea, a certain priest named Zechariah was serving in the course of Abijah. According to the custom of his priestly office, he was, at the time, burning

incense in the Temple when an angel appeared to him, announcing that his barren wife Elisabeth was going to have a child who they were to name John.[109]

Then:

Six months later, God sent the angel Gabriel to Nazareth, a city in Galilee, to a virgin who was engaged to Joseph, of the House of David; her name was Mary.[110]

It was then that the angel told her she'd soon conceive and give birth to a Child Who they should call Jesus.[111] Then, when Mary asked how this could even be possible, seeing she'd yet to have a physical relationship with a man, the angel replied simply:

The Holy Spirit will come upon you, and the Child you'll give birth to is going to be called the Son of God.[112]

Then notice what the angel declared in the next verse:

And see how your cousin Elisabeth has also conceived a son in her old age, she who is now in her sixth month of pregnancy—all this to the one who they used to call barren, because with God nothing is impossible.[113]

So, thanks to this series of verses, Luke has provided enough numerical values from which even the most rudimentary student of math can deduce the time of year that Jesus was born. The solution to this all-important equation rests on the figures derived from the following historical facts.

According to Jewish scholars, the priestly period of Abijah occurred sometime between mid-June and early July, which would place the conception of Jesus approximately six months later. That would mean conception occurred sometime between mid-December and early January. Thus, John would've been born sometime between mid-March and early April, and Jesus would've been born six months after that, sometime between mid-September, at the onset of the fall of the year, and early October.

So again, *The Bible* proves itself capable of standing up to any form of scrutiny. And in the end, what we find is, all this talk about Jesus

---

[109] *Luke* 1: 5-13
[110] Ibid. 1: 26-27
[111] Ibid. 1:31
[112] Ibid. 1:34-35
[113] Ibid. 1:36-37

being just another messianic wanna-be, born one among many on the Winter Solstice, is, itself, the product of an overactive imagination bent on undermining the uniqueness of Christ.

There you have it, then: Yet another germ of truth in *The Bible*, which over the course of time was distorted into a confused blend of fact and fiction. In this case, we have a timeless tale, beautifully conceived, of God's salvation offered to a dying race, the story of the Son of God taking on flesh and blood to rescue His rebellious creation through His own sacrificial death. Yet ultimately the historical events that confirm God's faithfulness regarding the Advent of Christ are now virtually indistinguishable from the counterfeit legends surrounding the pagan worship of the Sun-god.

The culprit in this whole affair, however, is ironically not one but two—those who seek to dethrone Christ as well as those who desire only to enthrone Him. There are those who actively spread their disinformation that claims that Jesus is nothing more than an imaginative product of centuries of legends ... and there are those who inadvertently make those legends all the more effective by their tacit disregard for a genuine depiction of the birth of the long-awaited Coming One.

Though in the end, there's no power on Earth that can resist the goodness and light of the Savior—the mercy mild, heralding the glory of the newborn King—Whose birth as it turns out occurred in the fall of the year, and not, as traditions would have us believe, on December 25th.

Misconception #36

Jesus Never Answered Pilate's Question: "What is Truth?"

AS THE STORY GOES: The prisoner stood, head hanging in quiet submission, as Pontius Pilate, the Roman governor, grilled him about his role in the most recent Judean uprising. Rumor had it that the man before him was not only trying to usurp the throne of Herod Antipas, but he was also trying to stir up an insurrection amongst the Jewish zealots under his jurisdiction.

But as far as Pilate was concerned, this vagabond—what was his name again, Jesus of Nazareth?—was interfering with the one thing that mattered most to him, the only thing. So, as the governor prodded his prisoner, he was far less concerned with the religious implications of the rumors swirling about the city. His primary concern was with the civil order that Tiberius Caesar himself had commissioned him to uphold.

A brutal mercenary, Pilate had already quelled several religious skirmishes in his territory; and this one would prove to be no different from the rest. It would be crushed at all cost, if not for the sake of Rome, then certainly for the sake of his own career. No time for chit-chat, Pilate came right out and asked Jesus the most important question on his mind: "Are you really the king of the Jews?"

But Jesus understood what He was up against. He knew Pilate was nothing more than a cutthroat politician; and the last thing He was going to do was to engage with him on his level. Pilate may have been skilled at this sort of thing, but Jesus was even better prepared to extinguish his kind of fiery temperament. Looking up at His interrogator, Jesus calmly replied, "Who wants to know? Are you asking for yourself? Or have others told you about Me?"

"Who me?" blurted Pilate. "What—you think I'm a Jew?" Fiercely eyeing his quarry, the malignant governor tried to stay on top of the situation. Far be it for this nobody from a backwash like Nazareth to get the best of him. "Your own people delivered you into my hands. The priests accuse you of crimes against the state. What have you done, anyway?"

Still, Jesus remained unruffled. "My kingdom is not of this world,"

He said, staring back at Pilate, with eyes that eerily bored into the irate governor. "If it were, My servants would be fighting for Me even as we speak, and the Jewish authorities would never have been able to hand Me over to you. But as it is, My kingdom is not of this place."

The fire in Pilate's eyes suddenly dimmed; but as to why, he couldn't say. Was it the serene calmness of his prisoner, even as he belligerently stared him down? Or was it something altogether different? He tried his best to conceal his confusion. "Then you are a king," he sputtered through clinched teeth. "Tell me now. Are you? Or aren't you?"

As gently as a summer breeze, Jesus smiled back at his captor, as if they'd been friends all their lives. "There, you see: You said it yourself. Even as you speak it, you know it's true. You say I'm a king, because that's the sole reason for which I was born. I came into this world to bear witness to the truth, and everyone who is of the truth hears My voice."

Then, just as gently, Pilate responded, defeated, worn down by his prisoner's solemn countenance. "Truth? Tell me, then. What is truth?"

It's then that the canonical account of Scripture tells us Jesus fell strangely silent, offering no reply to the governor's question.

"Why won't you answer me?" asked Pilate.

For several agonizing moments, Jesus just stared back at His interrogator without even blinking.

Pilate clenched his fist, as much in frustration as in anger. "Are you just going to stand there? Don't you know I have the power to release you or have you crucified?"

"But don't you see?" Jesus finally said. "You only have power over Me because it's been given to you from above; therefore the one who handed Me over to you is guilty of an even greater sin."

Shaking his head, the bewildered governor wiped his weary brow and exhaled loudly. He turned suddenly on his heels, exited the room, and stepped into the hallway, where he stood face to face with a group of black-robed Jewish leaders. "It's sheer madness, I tell you," Pilate growled. "I've never seen anything like it. This man has done nothing that warrants a charge of guilt, and yet—"

"I beg your pardon, Governor," snapped Caiaphas, the high priest at Jerusalem. "You couldn't be more wrong. This man is a subversive of the highest order; he has the entire city in an uproar. Have you forgotten what happened the last time these people you're supposed to govern started a riot? If it happens again, sir, and Caesar finds out you stood by and did nothing to prevent it, I guarantee you'll suffer the consequences!"

Pilate's eyes thinned and he inhaled slowly, simmering with

resentment at the mere thought. The only thing he hated more than having to corral this bunch of zealous Jews was having the leader of these zealots best him in a contest of wills. So, as much as he hated to agree with Caiaphas' appraisal of the situation, Pilate did agree that something had to be done to dispel the people before another riot ensued. As a minion of Rome, Pilate had one duty above all others: To maintain the civil order of his territory ... no matter the cost. His only choice, then, was to hand Jesus over to the angry mob, who executed Him, much to the chagrin of even a cutthroat politician like Pontius Pilate.[114]

So goes the story, as they say, right?

Okay, so what happened here? Let me get this straight: Jesus—the Man of Truth, born into the world with the sole purpose of testifying to the truth—refused to answer Pilate's question: "What is truth?"

Does that even make sense?

You mean, just when it seemed like Jesus had His interrogator right where He wanted him, just when He had reduced the previously rabid governor to putty in His hands, He could've answered Pilate's question. But He didn't.

Why? Was it because Jesus was more interested in dying for the cause than living for it? Was He worried that had He answered such a pivotal question He might have persuaded Pilate to switch sides and release Him? Had He answered the question, considering Pilate's new state of mind, would Jesus have found Himself at cross-purposes with the will of His Father?

I suppose all of these are valid points indeed. But actually, they turn out to be moot points when one considers another source of biblical truth that we've become familiar with in this series of essays. I'm talking about the apocryphal literature, of course—more specifically, a text known as *The Gospel of Nicodemus*, formerly called *The Acts of Pontius Pilate*.

In this remarkable work, we discover a parallel narrative that covers the exact same period in the life of Jesus. In the third chapter of *Nicodemus*, we find the same conversation in John's Gospel, repeated almost word for word; yet it contains one twist that puts a whole new spin on the conversation.

Instead of portraying Jesus as refusing to answer Pilate's question, this narrative reveals something altogether different. In this version, when the governor asked, "What is truth?" he received a truly provocative response.

"Truth," said Jesus, quite matter-of-factly, "is from Heaven."

---

[114] *John* 18:33-40, 19:1-16

To which a disappointed Pilate replied, "So truth is not of this Earth; is it that?"

Undaunted, Jesus looked at the crestfallen governor squarely in the eye and, with a wry smile, said: "Don't be too sure of yourself, my friend. Truth exists on this Earth. That is, it does for those who are governed by truth and who make right decisions because of that truth."[115]

How interesting is that? Now that sounds more like the Jesus I read about in *The Bible*—unflinching, uncompromising, unabashed.

So what gives? Why does the canonical record leave this part of the story out? And more importantly, am I the only person to have read the Apostle John's account and wondered: Why didn't Jesus answer that question? How could He remain silent on such an important issue? How could He have acted so indifferently?

I suppose the most obvious answer that comes to mind is, in a very real sense, John was using Pilate as a stand-in for all mankind, who also stand bewildered as to why Jesus refused to answer him. And because there is no response for Pilate, we, too, along with him, have no concrete answer to such a momentous question.

But personally, I've always been left with the sneaking suspicion that something was missing from this account.

But what? And more importantly, why?

Only when we're willing to "read between the lines," as it were, of the canonical record, which can only be done with the aid of the apocryphal literature, do we finally begin to come to a genuine insight concerning this enigmatic scene.

In light of the alternate version in *The Gospel of Nicodemus*, we begin to see the canonical text differently. Unlike the record in John's Gospel, Nicodemus has Jesus answering Pilate's question with a reasonable and intelligent answer. The only problem: Pilate never took His answer to heart. As profound as it was, the answer didn't move him to act on it. And by not acting, Pilate perfectly illustrated what Jesus had described: "Truth exists on the Earth, but it does so only for those who make correct decisions based on that truth." Thus, for those who refuse to act on truth, truth does not exist.

Seen this way, we can no longer assume that this most important of all questions never received an answer just because we're only familiar with this conversation as seen through the eyes of John. We now know, by looking at the apocryphal record, the real picture is more like that of a parent who's answered a rebellious teenager's tricky question, but because the teenager clearly has no intention of acting

---

[115] *Nicodemus* 3:11-14

upon the answer given, the parent must choose a different approach.

No longer can we continue to entertain the idea that Pilate asked this question to a seemingly indifferent Savior. What becomes apparent, then, is John must have purposely condensed the conversation between Jesus and Pilate. Might this be a case of what I suggested earlier, concerning John's view of God's purpose for Pilate in all of this? Could it be that in asking the question, "What is truth?" Pilate really was acting as a stand-in for all mankind?

If so, then we might just be seeing the following scenario: Pilate, like us, wants to know the same thing, but sadly, like Pilate, we, too, are just as likely to balk at the very answer we think we want to hear.

In the end, what we see, in John's rendition of this scene, is a case in which John, knowing all too that we won't respond to Jesus' answer any more than Pilate did, he simply deleted His response as though He'd never answered it in the first place. Because, as in the case of truth: For those who don't act on the answer, the answer doesn't exist.

Misconception #35

The Call of Christ Comes Unexpectedly and Unannounced

AS IF TRADITION itself weren't potent enough, add to that the power of melodrama, and together you have two of the most irresistible weapons in the arsenal of anyone looking to create a great misconception of *The Bible*.

In this case, what we have is an itinerant preacher by the name of Jesus of Nazareth Who's going about the Judean countryside and indiscriminately challenging people to join His ministry. As Scripture portrays it:

> Jesus was walking by the Sea of Galilee, when He saw Peter and his brother Andrew fishing. And Jesus said, "Follow Me, and I'll make you fishers of men."
>
> Immediately, the two of them left their nets and began following Him.
>
> From there, Jesus continued on His way, finding two more brothers, James and John, the sons of Zebedee, who were sitting in a ship with their father as they mended their nets. He called out to them, and immediately they put down their nets and followed Him.[116]

Then, later:

> Jesus saw a man named Matthew, who was sitting in the seat of the tax collector, and He said to him: "Follow Me."
>
> So Matthew got up and followed Jesus.[117]

Now, upon reading this, we naturally get the impression that Jesus is just wandering about, haphazardly tossing out His divine calling card to whomever He happens to meet. Someone strikes His fancy, He blurts out an invitation to follow Him in His spiritual quest, and that person instantly drops everything after but a single, brief encounter with this mysterious yet charismatic stranger. Abandoning their old

---

[116] *Matthew* 4:18-22; *Mark* 1:16-20

[117] *Matthew* 9:9; *Mark* 2:14

lives, these men, at a moment's notice, decide to follow Jesus, never once questioning the motives of this Man Who's demanding such an apparently hasty decision from them. Pretty gutsy stuff, if you ask me.

Still, I wonder: Did it really happen the way tradition has portrayed it for so many centuries? Did they all just drop everything that suddenly?

"Of course it happened that way," you'd insist, "because Scripture uses the word 'immediately' in describing their reaction to Jesus, doesn't it?"

"Well, yes, I do admit that it does; but as usual, I still can't help thinking there's something missing here. As usual, I find it so tempting to disagree with the traditional interpretation of events as they've been neatly handed down to us."

"But why?" you may ask. "Why are you always so prone to doubt the authenticity of *The Bible*?"

To which I'd reply, "It's not Scripture that I doubt. What I'm questioning is the view that when, as potential converts of Christianity—which the twelve disciples obviously were—we're expected to drop everything at the proverbial 'drop of hat.' I'm questioning the assumption that anyone who wishes to follow Christ must do so with the same reckless abandon as these first converts. And I am especially questioning the attitude that, in order to properly follow Christ, we must do so with a kind of 'blind' faith."

According to this view, it seems as though we're only acceptable in His sight if we throw away everything of our earthly life and hurl ourselves into the void, and all because that's the way the early disciples did it. That's what I'm questioning—something that, quite frankly, amounts to an over-simplified, romanticized view of accepting the call of Christ.

Now, again, before anyone accuses me of heresy because I seem to be disagreeing with the clear-cut demands of Jesus, let's first review this traditional scenario in light of the three laws of disinformation. In other words, let's revisit the total narrative of these encounters with Jesus in order to provide the context to His call of the disciples. Fair enough? Good, then let's do just that.

Naturally, our first order of business is to see if there are any variations of this rendition of history amongst the gospel writers themselves. Fortunately, we do find such a thing in Mark's account.

Prior to the call of Matthew, we read that news began to circulate about what Jesus was doing in the cities around Galilee, where His deeds of healing had become so famous He could no longer enter any city without great fanfare.[118] When Jesus decided to visit Capernaum, the crowds surrounding Him were so dense there was hardly room enough to stand.

Meanwhile, four men brought their friend who was sick with the palsy, hoping Jesus would heal him, too. But because the room was so crowded, the men had to break a hole in the roof in order to lower their bedridden friend into the presence of Jesus, Who was so impressed with their faith He immediately healed the man. Stunned, everyone watched as the man got up under his own strength, picked up his bed, and walked out of the room, as if he'd never been sick at all.

From there, Jesus went to the seaside, teaching the crowds along the way. This was when He spotted Matthew doing his job of tax collecting, and when He invited him to drop everything he was doing to follow Him.[119]

The reason I mention all this is to set the scene in which this call of Christ took place. If you notice, it didn't occur, as tradition is so fond of portraying, in a vacuum, as if Matthew had been ignorant of Jesus' reputation as a powerful healer, and as if he'd never heard any of His teachings. If that had been the case, then, yes, dropping everything to follow Jesus could be perceived as a daring and heroic move by someone who was making a decent living just sitting around collecting taxes. But that's not what the context of Mark's Gospel presents to us.

According to it, Matthew knew exactly what Jesus was doing and teaching, so that when he was invited to follow Him, he chose to do so with an acute awareness of Who he was getting involved with. This isn't to say that Matthew had any idea as to the repercussions of following Jesus, as this is something for which none of us are ever prepared. But it does demonstrate he wasn't acting impulsively, as tradition would have us believe.

What's more, Mark continued with this idea in the next chapter when he described how tremendous crowds would gather about Jesus, having heard about the incredible things He'd been doing. And because so many sick people were being healed simply by touching Him, the crowd would press into Him, forcing Jesus to teach the multitudes from a small ship docked at the seashore.

Mark even recorded that whenever a person possessed by a demon would pass by, they'd fall at His feet, acknowledging that He was the Son of God. It was within this unique context, then, that Mark said Jesus called His twelve disciples. Again, the picture that Mark is creating for us is one in which Jesus was calling people who were all

---

[118] *Mark* 1:45
[119] Ibid. 2:1-14

fully aware of the astounding nature of the One Who was calling them, and not of people who were ignorant of the circumstances that surrounded Him.

In short, everyone who Jesus invites to follow Him knows exactly Who they're being asked to follow, and why.

This same idea was confirmed by Jesus in His famous discourse about the Good Shepherd. The sheep don't ignorantly follow the shepherd; they do so because they know His voice, whereas others they won't follow because they don't recognize the voice of a stranger.[120] Said Jesus:

> I am the Good Shepherd. I know My sheep, and they know Me… My sheep hear My voice … and they follow Me.[121]

So you see, if we're to believe Jesus, then it should be obvious that whenever He calls someone into a relationship with Him, He does so with their complete understanding. He doesn't blindside them or catch them unprepared. He's taught them, He's touched their heart, their soul, and, if need be, their body, and now He's laying claim to the reins of their life. After everything He's done to that point, He's now challenging them to acknowledge that it's been His voice that they've been hearing all along.

To believe otherwise would be to ignore what the entire context of Scripture presents, even as the psalmist wrote centuries before the Advent of Christ: "You've possessed my reins, having covered me in my mother's womb."[122]

So, considering all this scriptural evidence, why would anyone believe that the call of Christ would come to someone, as if that person had unwittingly stumbled into some kind of cosmic surprise party?

Well, let's see; how about because centuries of church tradition have led us to believe in such melodramatic nonsense? After a lifetime of having been bombarded with verses that are constantly being quoted out of context, it's no wonder that most people misinterpret what *The Bible* has to say on this subject. And remember, one only needs to extract a few verses to create a truly effective disinformation strategy.

For example, when Jesus asked a man to follow Him, he asked if he could first be allowed to bury his father; to which Jesus famously replied, "Let the dead bury the dead."[123] Then, when Jesus asked another man to follow Him, he agreed to do so but asked for

---

[120] *John* 10:4-5

[121] Ibid. 10:14, 27

[122] *Psalm* 139:13

[123] *Matthew* 8:22; *Luke* 9:60

permission to first say goodbye to his family, which prompted Jesus to say, "No one who puts his hand to the plow and then looks back is fit for the Kingdom of God."[124]

Certainly these verses do seem to support the view that Jesus caught all these people off guard when He called them—when seen in isolation, that is. But remember, none of them were living in a cave somewhere, ignorant of the Man Who had addressed them. Based on a contextual understanding of the events surrounding them, it's not hard to imagine that every one of these men had already encountered Jesus at some point, and that each of them had had some desire to leave their old lives in order to follow Him. More than likely, what we're seeing is simply the moment of decision when Matthew and Luke wrote about them.

Now, this doesn't mean that when God does outwardly call someone to His service that it doesn't look like a complete surprise to everyone else. This is, unfortunately, why it's so easy for these stories to be removed from their biblical context and made to appear as though they exist only in their isolated forms.

Fortunately, though, we can restore the context of these stories by simply taking the time to review them in their totality. Then, and only then, are we able to see what nonsense it is to think that, when *The Bible* depicts Christ as calling His chosen ones, this was the first time they'd ever encountered Jesus. In fact, to believe otherwise, one would have to deny what's clearly written about in the books of *Hebrews* and *Romans*, which both describe a God Who's always been speaking to humanity about the Coming One.

> God, Who's spoken to us by the prophets throughout many different eras and in many different ways, has in these last days spoken to us by his Son, Whom He's appointed heir of all things, by Whom He also created the Universe.[125]

And:

> Because since the creation of the world, the invisible things of God have been clearly seen, having been made understandable by the things that were created, even God Himself and His eternal power, so that everyone is without excuse.[126]

And again:

---

[124] *Luke* 9:62

[125] *Hebrews* 1:1-2

[126] *Romans* 1:20

THE CALL OF CHRIST COMES UNEXPECTEDLY

To the ones whom God foreknew, He also predestined to be conformed to the image of His Son so that He might be the firstborn of many children. Moreover, to those He predestined, He called; and to those He called, He also justified by faith; and to those He justified, He glorified.[127]

Based on the testimony of these passages, then, it's obvious that when God calls someone, it's done with a great deal more preparation and deliberation than has previously been understood. As such, one thing is certain beyond a doubt: From time immemorial, there's never been a time when the deliverance of Christ wasn't unfolding in the sight of all humanity, until "the call" comes to whomever it will.

Misconception #34

Not Even God Can Find the Lost Tribes of Israel

BUT KING SOLOMON loved many strange women;[128] so says *The Bible*, speaking of the same man who had once been called the wisest man in the world.

The Wisdom of Solomon was said to have been as measureless as the sand on the seashore, greater than all the wisdom of the East, greater than all of Egypt. He was said to have written three hundred proverbs and more than a thousand songs. Solomon was so wise, in fact, that people from every nation in the ancient world came to hear him speak, among them, the fabled Queen of Sheba.[129] Solomon, son of David, and builder of the splendors of the Temple of God at Jerusalem; Solomon, the man who loved many strange women, and whose many wives eventually turned his heart after other gods.[130]

So the Lord became angry with Solomon, because in his old age his heart turned away from the God of Israel, so He told him:

Because you've done this thing ... I will tear the kingdom away from you and give it to one of your own officials. But

---

[127] *Romans* 8:29-30
[128] *First Kings* 11:1
[129] Ibid. 4:29-34; 10:1-13
[130] Ibid. 11:4

for the sake of your father David, I won't do this while you're alive, but I'll tear it out of the hand of your son.

Still, I won't tear the whole kingdom from him, but I'll give him one tribe for My servant David's sake and for the sake of Jerusalem, which I've chosen.[131]

In this way, Solomon went from being the wisest man in the world, unmatched in wealth, power, and prestige, to the man who was responsible for dividing the kingdom of Israel that had stood united for more than a hundred years. Thus, the stage was set for a new chapter in the drama of God's people.

And what a drama it's been, from the moment that Moses led the Israelites through the parted Red Sea, through forty years of wandering through the Wilderness en route to their new home, with just a slight detour at Mount Sinai along the way. Then, triumphantly entering the Promised Land after having conquered the land under the leadership of Joshua, the Israelites settled there—a chosen people separated to their God.

At first, they were ruled by a series of judges, by the likes of Gideon, Jephthah, and Samson. But afterward, the people demanded a king to rule over them; and although God preferred being their King, He eventually relented and provided them with a dynasty of human kings—first Saul, then David, then his son Solomon.

And although the people of Israel seemed at first to have gotten what they'd wished for, there was never a time in the history of these kings that there wasn't some form of controversy. The issue came down to just one thing: Could a nation borne by the miraculous intervention of a Supreme Being be ruled by that same Deity—whether by His own hand or through some human intermediary?

To this day, sadly, the answer remains very much in doubt.

Then, sometime in the days after Solomon had received word that God would be dividing the kingdom, one of his officials by the name of Jeroboam had been traveling just outside of Jerusalem. As it turns out, this man had so impressed Solomon in a recent building project involving the walls of Jerusalem that the old king had put Jeroboam in charge of the entire working force of the tribes of Joseph.

This day, Jeroboam was strolling along, dressed in a new coat, feeling very satisfied about his new station in life, both courtesy of King Solomon himself, when suddenly a strange-looking fellow stepped up to him.

"Hello, Jeroboam," the strange man said. "I'm so glad, so glad I

---

[131] *First Kings* 11:9, 11-13

finally found you."

"Me? Why me?" replied Jeroboam, squinting his eyes in the harsh glare of the midday Sun, trying to size up this odd fellow as quickly as possible. "Who are you, anyway?"

"I am Ahijah ... from Shiloh... I'm called Ahijah, yes?"

Mulling this over for several moments, Jeroboam's eyes then lit up. "Ahijah ... ah, yes, of Shiloh, you say... Are you *the* Ahijah, then? Ahijah, the prophet?"

"I am, sir," Ahijah said, respectfully nodding his head.

Jeroboam nodded back. "So nice to meet you, my friend."

"You've heard about me, then? Is that what you're saying?"

"Certainly; who in Jerusalem hasn't?" Jeroboam replied, then suddenly growing uneasy. "Say, what's this all about, anyway?"

"I have message for you—that's what this is about."

"A message ... for me? From who?"

"The Holy One of Israel, that's who—the Lord God Himself!"

Stunned, Jeroboam's eyes thinned. "The Lord God? What on Earth are you talking about? What message?"

Without warning, Ahijah thrust his hands forward and grabbed hold of Jeroboam's new coat.

"For God's sake, man!" Jeroboam snorted. "What are you doing? Keep your hands off me!"

A struggled then ensued as each man jockeyed for position, but clearly this odd-looking fellow was much stronger than Jeroboam had anticipated and before he knew it, the man—this prophet of God?—had removed his coat. And before Jeroboam could say another word, Ahijah started tearing the coat to pieces right before his gaping eyes.

"You crazy fool!" barked Jeroboam. "That was a brand-new coat! King Solomon just gave it to me! Have you lost your mind?"

Tearing the coat into a dozen pieces, Ahijah handed Jeroboam most of them. "Here; you take ten pieces for yourself. This is what the Lord says: I'm going to tear the kingdom out of Solomon's hand and give you ten tribes." Ahijah then held up the last two pieces in his hand for Jeroboam to see. "But for the sake of My servant David and My city Jerusalem, his son will get one tribe. As for you, Jeroboam, I'm making you king over Israel; and if you obey Me as David did, I'll be with you. And in the days to come, you watch: I'll build you a dynasty as enduring as the one I built for David."[132]

In this most peculiar way, then, God, through the prophet Ahijah, sparked off the revolution that would divide the kingdom, around 900 B.C., with the ten tribes of Israel to the north and the two tribes of

---

[132] *First Kings* 11:29-38

Judah to the south.

For the next two hundred years, the northern kingdom of Israel would see the rise and fall of nineteen kings, springing from nine different dynastic families. The southern kingdom of Judah would follow a much different pattern, though just as troublesome. For more than three hundred years, they would see the ascension of nineteen kings and one queen, all originating from the line of David.

Eventually, as a form of divine punishment, both kingdoms were destroyed by invading armies, with the House of Israel being carried away by the Assyrians around 722 B.C. and the House of Judah, by the Babylonians around 586 B.C. But whereas the House of Judah remained fairly intact during their Babylonian captivity, it was the unique fate of the House of Israel to receive the specific judgment of being scattered throughout the nations. That's when, according to the traditional view of history, the northern ten tribes seemed to vanish from the face of the Earth, and why they became known ever after as the Lost Tribes of Israel.

But is that really the final chapter to the story? Is tradition correct in its view that these so-called "lost tribes" are gone forever, never to be seen or heard from again? Or, as we've seen time and time again, does *The Bible* actually portray a far different picture?

As I see it, there are three questions we need to answer if we're to solve this age-old mystery. One, why did God scatter the House of Israel amongst the nations in the first place? Two, if these northern tribes were lost to history, does that mean God lost track of them, too? And three, is it God's intention that they remain lost forever?

First, let's look at what the Scriptures say about why God scattered the northern House of Israel. In *The Book of Leviticus*, we find the origin of God's intention toward them, when He said:

> I am the Lord your God, Who rescued you from Egypt so that you'd no longer be slaves to them... But if you resist My laws, hate My statutes, and scorn My judgments... I'll oppose you, and you'll be destroyed by your enemies. And if you refuse to obey Me, I'll punish you seven times more for your sins.[133]

This same idea repeats three more times, in the next ten verses, and then God said:

---

[133] *Leviticus* 26:13, 15, 17-18

And if, in spite of all these things, you still refuse to listen to Me ... then I'll scatter you among the heathen, and your cities will lie desolate.[134]

But why would God do something like that? Why doesn't He just punish the people and be done with it? Why does He have to remove them from the land, too? The following verses explain why.

Then the land will finally enjoy the Sabbaths as long as your land lies desolate and you remain in the land of your enemies.
As long as your land remains uninhabitable, then it will rest, even as it didn't rest during the time that you lived there.[135]

So, there's the answer to our first question. God scattered the people of Israel so the land would be able to fulfill His plan—in this case, concerning the much-misunderstood concept of the Sabbath rest, which typifies what *The Book of Hebrews* speaks of when it describes the rest that follows the work of faith.

We who have had faith have entered into that rest. Whereas God spoke in another place about the seventh day in this regard: "And God rested on the seventh day from all His works."
Therefore, there remains a rest for the people of God, because whoever enters into His rest has also ceased from his own works, just as God did from His.[136]

In other words, when God's people live according to the precepts of faith, they, too, can expect to rest in that accomplishment, even as God rested on the seventh day of His creation. This, then, is the true meaning of Sabbath rest.

The real significance of this is, for most of the time that the Children of Israel lived in Palestine, they'd lost sight of the true purpose for which God had placed them there. They weren't there simply for their own sakes; God had a much greater purpose in mind, a purpose they usually squandered. That's why God removed them from the land, so they might finally turn from their old ways of disobedience, which could only be done after they'd been carried away into captivity. Only then could the Israelites return to the kind of faith they'd all but forgotten about after so many years of false religion, fostered by the

---

[134] *Leviticus* 26:33

[135] Ibid. 26:34-35

[136] *Hebrews* 4:3-4, 10

belief that they'd always be God's darlings, no matter what they did to provoke Him.

The next question, then, is: Once the northern tribes of Israel were carried away into captivity, did God lose track of them in their lost condition? The prophet Amos gives us a hint of God's perspective of this global drama.

> See how I observe this sinful kingdom, having destroyed it from the face of the Earth, though I haven't utterly wiped out the House of Jacob. Look at how I've commanded, so that I'll sift the House of Israel throughout every nation, as corn is sifted in a sieve, yet I haven't lost track of a single grain.[137]

Based on this passage, then, it's obvious that just because history lost track of the Lost Tribes doesn't mean that God ever lost track of them. The prophet Hosea confirmed this, when he had God saying, "Israel isn't hidden from Me, for I see that she's defiled."[138]

In fact, God was so intent on Hosea conveying this message of Israel's defilement, He commanded him to do the unthinkable. Just as Ahijah had done before him, in making his point absolutely clear to Jeroboam by tearing his new coat into twelve pieces, God would, with Hosea, up the ante even further. The first thing the Lord did—to ram His message down the proverbial throat of an entire nation—was to have Hosea marry a prostitute! Then He had His prophet name his three children by this woman according to a specific aspect of the divine judgment that, because of their idolatry and disobedience, would soon overtake them.

> And Hosea's wife bore him a son whom he named Jezreel, because God said, "Soon I'll cause the kingdom of Israel to cease."
>
> Then his wife bore him a daughter whom he named Loruhamah, because God said, "I'll no longer have mercy on the House of Israel, but will allow them to be carried away into captivity."
>
> And finally, his wife gave birth to yet another son whom Hosea named Loammi, because God said, "You're no longer My people, and I won't be your God."[139]

So, if you think Jeroboam was shocked when Ahijah handed him ten pieces of what had just been his new coat, just imagine the stunned

---

[137] *Amos* 9:8-9

[138] *Hosea* 5:3

[139] Ibid. 1:3-9

look on the faces of those Israelites when they saw one of God's own prophets had married a whore—and had three kids by her, to boot! The only thing more shocking, I'm sure, would've been the look on any of the faces of those who'd come to understand what God was trying to tell them through Hosea's actions.

Fortunately for all involved, though, the story of Israel's disgrace was destined to not end on such a dismal note, because, as bizarre as it certainly appeared to the uninitiated, the Lord was still working out an important purpose in all of this. Just when all hope seemed lost, God interjected a remarkable twist to this ongoing drama—a grand soap opera of the ages, if you will. Without even pausing between sentences, Hosea then prophesied of the day when Israel's downfall would actually lead to a new day of hope and restoration. On the heels of the previous passages of doom, the prophet declared:

> Yet the number of the Children of Israel will be as the sand of the sea that cannot be measured or numbered, and someday, in the very place where it was said, "You're not My people," even there it will be said, "You are the children of the Living God."[140]

This, then, provides us with the answer to our third question: No, God doesn't intend for the northern kingdom of Israel to remain lost forever. Though once a disgrace among the nations of the world, Israel, the desolate, Israel, the scattered, will one day be the recipients of one of God's greatest acts of mercy and redemption.

"But when," you might ask, "will these lost tribes be rediscovered? Has it already happened? Will it occur in our lifetime? Or is it likely to occur at some future point in time?"

Believe it or not, the answer involves not so much the theology of *The Bible* but, rather, the science of archeology. It was during the mid-1800s that this amazing science of uncovering the past began to discover where in the world the Lost Tribes of Israel had disappeared to after they'd been taken into captivity.

As if from out of nowhere, the discoveries made famous by men like Henry Rawlinson and Austen Henry Layard began to blow the lid off the whereabouts of these long-lost people. Almost overnight, what had been considered merely myth began to, slowly but surely, edge its way into the arena of factual history.

Between 1835 and 1839, Rawlinson copied and translated an inscription on an ancient rock relief located in western Iran, which bore an account authored by Darius the Great, the Persian king best known

---

[140] *Hosea* 1:10

for his role in the rebuilding of Jerusalem after the Babylonian Captivity. It's this relief, known as the Behistun Inscription, which provided the linguistic keys to determine the historical roots of the Lost Tribes of Israel. On it, three parallel narratives, written in Persian, Babylonian, and Scythian, describe events in the history of these scattered tribes, giving historians their first glimpse into the much sought after jumping-off point of these mysterious people.

Next came Layard, who, in 1847, unearthed the Assyrian capital of Nineveh and with it the royal library of the Assyrian kings, containing a vast array of clay tablets. Written in the seventh century B.C., these tablets contained cuneiform texts referring to the captive Israelites. Tying together all the data gathered via these unparalleled feats of archeology, scholars soon learned that the people whom *The Bible* says were captured and relocated to Assyria had actually remained a distinct and vibrant people. In time, this new group, known as the *Skythai*, or Scythians, multiplied so quickly and exerted such an influence that, within a hundred years or so, they broke free from captivity to become the people that history now records as the *Keltoi*, or Celts, of Europe.

According to historians, the first reference to these *Keltoi* was by the Greek geographer Hecataeus in 571 B.C., who, in giving them this name, has provided us with a telling clue as to their true origins. To some it might seem incidental, but certainly not to those who believe that when the God of *The Bible* says something He means it. As it so happens, *Keltoi*, say these same historians, comes from the Indo-European root word *kel*, which means "hidden."

Of course, there are always those who'd insist that none of this is even possible because once God punished them they were supposed to remain hidden, to wander life ever after as outcasts among the nations into which they were scattered. But not according to the prophet Jeremiah, who saw a far different fate for them:

> For Israel is not forsaken, or Judah, of their God; though their land is full of guilt against the Holy One of Israel...
>
> You are My battle-axe and weapons of war, and with you, I'll break in pieces the nations. With you, I'll destroy kingdoms, and with you, I'll break in pieces the horse and the rider.[141]

Far from being timid nomads, the Celts were fierce warriors that swept across the European continent, in wave after irresistible wave, terrorizing even the legions of Rome. They eventually grew so plentiful

---

[141] *Jeremiah* 51:5, 20-21

that they split into innumerable factions—among them: Gauls, Goths, Picts, Angles, Saxons, and Jutes. As such, these prodigious nations—as populous "as the sand of the sea"—came to inhabit the whole of Europe, including Italy, France, Belgium, Brittany, Spain, Portugal, Germany, Holland, Denmark, Sweden, Norway, Finland, England, Wales, Scotland, and Ireland.

So much can be said about these vast migrations and the many volumes of scholarship concerning them that this work could never encompass it all. Suffice it to say, the cultural connections have been made, and they've been done by some of the most prolific scholars in the annals of history. For the sake of this essay, however, what we've provided still makes the point abundantly clear: Yes, God in His righteous indignation punished the northern House of Israel with dispersion. Yes, He even blinded them with a temporary form of "national amnesia," as it were. But never did He intend to leave them in a permanent state of derision and destitution. As depicted in His word of promise and as revealed through the timely establishment of the science of archeology, both bear witness to God's unique ability to guide and nurture those people who are called by His Name.

Thus, it appears the prophecy of Hosea has actually come true, and with it, another of the greatest misconceptions ever blamed on *The Bible* has come crashing down. After all, we only need to ask a series of questions to verify the preceding statements: Where did the message of Christianity spread like wildfire if not in every one of the nations just mentioned? And if not in those nations—though once hidden, yet restored in the fullness of time—then where else would you suggest that it was more fervently received? And if they did embrace the Gospel of Christ brought to them by ambassadors of truth like the Apostle Paul and his group, then what greater proof is there to verify the fulfillment of Hosea's prophecy?

As it was written, and as it undoubtedly came to pass:

> Yet the number of the Children of Israel will be as the sand of the sea, which cannot be measured or numbered. And someday, in the very place where it was said, "You're not My people," it will be said, "You are the children of the Living God."[142]

THIS CONCLUDES *Fish Tales, Reel One*. To read further, please refer to the next book in this series, entitled *Fish Tales (From the Belly of the*

---

[142] *Hosea* 1:10

Whale): Reel Two. Or, if you prefer, you can read the entire work, which contains all three reels in a single volume, by referring to *Fish Tales (From the Belly of the Whale): Fifty of the Greatest Misconceptions Ever Blamed on The Bible*. To get this publication, or an eBook version of this text, go to *The Lost Stories Channel* at loststorieschannel.com, or Amazon Books, Barnes and Noble, or Apple Books.

Additionally, for those of you who are so inclined, please post a positive review of this book on such websites as Amazon, Barnes and Noble, Apple, and Goodreads so that others might become aware of its valuable contents. Because this book was not published by a conglomerate-style publishing house, we rely more heavily on word-of-mouth to advertise its importance to others who, like yourself, are searching for books like this. Thank you for your support.

Coming Attractions

Reel Two: The Line #33-18

*DUE TO THE PERSONAL NATURE of Saving Grace, God
Can Save Only One Person at a Time*

*YOU HAVE TO DIE and Wait Hundreds of Years Before the
Church Can Declare You a Saint*

A CHRISTIAN'S MAIN TASK in Life to Care for the Poor and Needy

*THE STORY OF TWO MEN IN A BED, and Two Women at the Mill,
While Only One is Taken, is a Prophecy of the Rapture*

*WHEN JESUS SAID There'd be Many False Prophets in the Last Days
That Means There Won't be Any True Prophets Left*

GOD IS LOVE THEREFORE He Loves Everyone All the Time

*THE MEDIEVAL WORLD Believed the Earth was Flat, Stationary, and
the Center of the Universe Because The Bible Says So*

*THEOLOGY AND SCIENCE are Natural Enemies
Because of Their Inherent Incompatibility*

*GOD IS ANGRY AND VENGEFUL in The Old Testament But
is Loving and Merciful in The New Testament*

*THE CONCEPT OF Being "Born Again" is
Found Only in The New Testament*

HEAVEN, UNLIKE THE EARTH, is an Eternal Place

HELL, LIKE HEAVEN, is a Place of Perpetual Existence

*WHEN THE APOSTLE PETER Recognized Jesus was the Christ, Jesus
Declared He'd Build His Church on the Foundation of Peter*

*YOU KNOW THE DEVIL Loves to Possess Humans Because
Jesus Told Peter: "Get Behind Me, Satan"*

*THE VERSE: "BEHOLD, I Stand at the Door
and Knock" is Addressed to Sinners*

*NOBODY KNOWS THE DAY or the Hour of the Second
Coming of Christ, Not Even Jesus*

About the Author

FOR MORE than forty years, W. Kent Smith has immersed himself in the teachings of the greatest biblical scholars of the ages—William Barclay, C.S. Lewis, W. Gene Scott, *et al*. More importantly during that time, he has immersed himself in *The Bible* itself. Add to that, Kent's unique perspective on history, humanity, and life, and the result is a one-of-a-kind take on biblical history and theology. What that means to you as a fellow truth seeker is a message unhindered by many outmoded traditions of biblical interpretation.

Beholden to no deacon board or school of thought, Kent has remained free to tread where others are unwilling to tread, and because of that, a brand-new view of Scripture has emerged. Not some new revelation, mind you, in the sense of it being above and beyond *The Bible* itself. What we are talking about is a fresh understanding of what Scripture has been saying all along, one that's been hidden in plain sight, waiting for someone to connect the dots, to reveal a picture that's been lying dormant until now.

Kent lives in West Covina, California, an eastern suburb of Los Angeles. He can be contacted at wkent@loststorieschannel.com, or lodestarcinema@msn.com.

www.ingramcontent.com/pod-product-compliance
Lightning Source LLC
Chambersburg PA
CBHW072051290426
44110CB00014B/1634